Reading
with
Presence

MARILYN PRYLE

Reading
with
Presence

Crafting Mindful, Evidence-Based
Reading Responses

HEINEMANN
Portsmouth, NH

Heinemann
361 Hanover Street
Portsmouth, NH 03801–3912
www.heinemann.com

Offices and agents throughout the world

The author and publisher wish to thank those who have generously given permission to reprint borrowed material:

"exploration, risk, and failure are . . ." tweet by Kelly Gallagher. Copyright © 2016 by Kelly Gallagher. Reprinted by permission of the author.

Acknowledgments for borrowed material continue on page xii.

Library of Congress Cataloging-in-Publication Data
Names: Pryle, Marilyn Bogusch, author.
Title: Reading with presence : crafting mindful, evidence-based reading responses / Marilyn Pryle.
Description: Portsmouth, NH : Heinemann, [2018] | Includes bibliographical references.
Identifiers: LCCN 2018017741 | ISBN 9780325088679
Subjects: LCSH: Reading (Secondary). | Reading comprehension—Study and teaching (Secondary).
  | Reader-response criticism. | Literature—Study and teaching (Secondary). | English language—
  Composition and exercises—Study and teaching (Secondary).
Classification: LCC LB1632 .P78 2018 | DDC 418/.40712 2 23

LC record available at https://lccn.loc.gov/2018017741

Editor: Katie Wood Ray
Production: Vicki Kasabian
Cover design: Suzanne Heiser
Cover images: © huePhotography / Getty Images (*books on beach*); © Sam Cole / EyeEm /
          Getty Images (*sand*)
Interior design: Monica Ann Crigler
Typesetter: Kim Arney
Manufacturing: Steve Bernier

Printed in the United States of America on acid-free paper
22 21 20 19 18   CGB   1 2 3 4 5

For Tim, who makes space for me to be present

Contents

Foreword

Years ago I held a series of workshops on writing for faculty at the University of New Hampshire. It was a heady experience—to work with brilliant leaders in oceanography, physics, and business. One thing they all had in common was their disappointment with the writing of their students. Many blamed the English Department for not preparing students for their courses, and more specifically they blamed me because I directed the first-year writing program.

I had them all bring in a writing assignment, and then I asked them to read it carefully and circle the key word—the verb that indicated the basic operation they wanted students to perform. It might be *discuss* or *analyze* or *interpret*. It might be *compare and contrast*, one of the most confusing directions: isn't contrasting a form of comparing (or comparing a form of contrasting)?

Once they had the word circled, I asked them if they felt that students knew what they meant by that word. Did students understand the mental operations—the process—for accomplishing it? Or was it a code word for a process that might be habitual for the teacher but foreign to the student, who then fell back on summarizing? Mike Rose has called this error in instruction "assumptive teaching"—assuming that simply by naming a mental operation, the student can do it. A perpetual task for any teacher is to crack open processes that are virtually automatic to us but not to our students.

The great virtue of *Reading with Presence* is its precision, the way Marilyn Pryle *names* the types of reading responses—and makes them manageable and accessible to students. Whenever I see exemplars of academic writing—such as the accomplished papers that appear in the appendices to the Common Core State Standards—I think, *Great, but how do students get there?* How do they develop familiarity with the various moves of academic writing? For example, how do they learn to quote effectively? Raise nonobvious questions? This book shows a pathway to proficiency.

There are four nonnegotiables in the reading responses Marilyn uses—students choose a category of response, use an original thought (i.e., not a summary), cite the text at least once, and write a minimum of a five-sentence paragraph. The categories she lays out—thirty-eight in all—build from more basic responses like stating and supporting an opinion to more sophisticated ones like seeing archetypes in literature or examining craft. Students can always choose the type of response to write, but they are encouraged to expand their repertoire—and to reflect on their own reading processes—over time.

As I see it, Pryle provides a manageable entry point for all students, a virtual ticket of admission that all can purchase. She invites students out of hiding. And as we all know there are two basic forms of hiding when it comes to analysis of literature—summary and silence. She asks them to *think*, even if it is nothing more than to have an impression of a character and a reason for that impression.

The book also shows a way to break the frustrating dynamic of the typical class discussion. Even "good" discussions tend to be dominated by a few students, almost always less than half the class. The longer the silent half remains silent, the more difficult it is for them to speak. In the rare occasions when a silent student finds the courage to speak, the reaction is something like "Wow, you have a voice." That sudden spotlight can be unnerving. But in my own sad experience, once this dynamic is set, it is hard to break. Silence soon becomes part of a student's identity. By having something in writing, all students are prepared for class discussion—everyone can enter in. Everyone has a ticket. And as students hear other students, using other categories of response, they can expand their own repertoire.

Another virtue of this approach is the sheer amount of practice students get. There is the old joke about the tourist in New York City who asks a local, "How do you get to Carnegie Hall?" And the local responds, "Practice." In my view, students are often asked to write longer papers with too little practice writing shorter ones, where they can develop the moves of response. The results are wooden formulaic essays, devoid of what Pryle calls *presence*, of real engagement. As I read this book, I could almost feel students becoming more familiar and at ease with these moves.

Everyone has probably heard another old story, of the tourist, lost in the backroads of Maine, who goes up to a farmhouse and asks an old Mainer, "How do I get to Portland?" And the farmer replies, "You can't get there from here." It often seems that way with analytic writing. It is often difficult to imagine (without rigid formulas) how students can move from where they are to the longer papers they will need to write. This book shows a way forward, with invitations wide enough, attractive enough, and manageable enough—that students will, I believe, decide they no longer need to hide.

—Thomas Newkirk

Acknowledgments

Teaching ideas are nothing without students who are willing to try them. First and foremost, I am deeply grateful for the many students who have passed through my classroom and entrusted me with their intellectual and personal growth. This includes students from over a decade ago at East Middle School in Braintree, Massachusetts, where I began experimenting with the Reading Response method described here, and also the students from Abington Heights High School in Clarks Summit, Pennsylvania, where I have taught for the past eight years. I am especially grateful to the class of 2019 at Abington, who were in my sophomore classes the year I wrote this book. To all students: I am humbled by your trust, openness, intellect, and heart.

I have also been privileged to work with colleagues who have been eager to try new ideas and work together. These include Rae Rudzinski, Andrea Bartlett, and Mike Stewart, whose students' work appears in this book. Thank you, friends, for your support and feedback, and for being so generous with your own classrooms.

When school leadership not only allows but encourages teachers to take risks, powerful results happen. I am grateful to Vicki Jones, Andy Snyder, Pam Murray, Mike Connelly, Michael Mahon, and the late Tom Quinn for cheering on my endeavors with confidence and enthusiasm.

My editor, Katie Wood Ray, saw the truest potential of this book even before I saw it; her vision, knowledge, craft, and belief in me has made me a deeper thinker and stronger teacher. I am more worthy of the profession after living through this experience with her. I am also incredibly grateful to be a part of Heinemann, and for the work of Edie Quinn Davis, Vicki Kasabian, Suzanne Heiser, Monica A. Crigler, Steve Bernier, Lynette Winegarner, Kim Cahill, and Brett Whitmarsh.

My parents, Ernest and Patricia Bogusch, taught me to love learning early on, and because of that, I teach. I am grateful for their dedication to my own education and growth, but even more so for their vision of what really matters in this life.

For me, writing happens anywhere and everywhere—in the early mornings and late at night, on marathon Sundays, on beach vacations, in hotels at national monuments, during drives through the desert. My husband, Tim, and our sons, Gavin and Tiernan, support me in all of it. I have come to understand that one of the greatest acts of love is to create space for another to do what brings joy. In that, I have been loved beyond measure, and am grateful beyond words.

Reading
with
Presence

Part One

Reading Responses as Classroom Practice

made it through school without ever really having to open my mouth. It was a pattern that began in grade school and continued into college. I raised my hand so rarely that once, in sixth grade, after I had been absent for a day or two and got up the nerve to ask a question in class, the teacher later pulled me aside to thank me for the question and encourage me to ask more. She even gave me a sticker! I felt so proud in that moment—I remember it to this day. And despite my wonderful teacher's best intentions (thank you, Mrs. Stanton!), her pep talk wasn't enough to change my deepest beliefs: I was deathly afraid of being wrong, of looking stupid, of speaking up at all. I didn't even think it was my role as a student to think my own thoughts—my job was to absorb enough of what was being projected to get good grades on the test. And that I did, though I never thought I was smart. Other kids in the class were clearly smart, but not me; I was just doing what was expected, without any real investment in the content.

I took honors courses in high school, but again, compliantly, fearfully at times, putting my time in and not identifying with the smart students. I was seldom called on, and when I was, it was for a one-word, clear-cut answer. I was one of those quiet kids that did her work and didn't cause trouble. I didn't believe I had a voice or a stake in my learning, but I also didn't realize those things were even possible. In class, I often daydreamed. For quizzes and tests, I crammed the necessary information. I never read with my heart. In the end, I graduated in the top 10 percent of my class and got into an honors program at the college I chose to attend.

In most of my college classes, I was able to continue as normal, hanging back, not wanting to be wrong, and not connecting. Others, though, weren't so easy. One day, one of my professors wouldn't let me off the hook. He called on me to comment about the poem we had read the night before, and I was simply too terrified to put forth a thought about it. So I replied in my usual way: "I don't know."

"What do you mean, you don't know? What do you think?" he pressed.

"I . . . I don't really know." Mortification.

"Did you read it?"

"Yes."

"Then you must have a thought. What did you think about it?"

"I, uh . . ." But I was frozen. My brain locked. The teacher grew impatient and called on someone else, who gave some easy answer about the role of imagery in the poem, an answer which the teacher praised. *I could have said that!* I thought to myself. I didn't realize he would have eagerly accepted something I thought was obvious. I thought he wanted to be dazzled with the meaning of life. In an awkward twist of fate, we boarded the same elevator after class. When the doors closed, he said, "Do you understand that you can't just say, 'I don't know'? You've got to have something to say. You have to speak."

"Yes," I said, wanting to vaporize through the seam of the elevator doors. I understood.

I never forgot that moment. It changed me: Slowly, I began to speak up, to say out loud the connections I made in my mind, the details I noticed in a text, the questions I had, and eventually, the opinions I felt. I already knew I wanted to be a teacher, and I appreciated what my professor had done, but I also knew I never wanted a student to feel like I had felt—dumb despite having understood the reading, and then ashamed for not being able to speak. Of course, I had needed a wake-up call. But I wondered: What could I do to help my future students believe they had something to say, even if it were a seemingly smaller detail? How could I make all students feel like they had something to bring to the discussion, and even feel this way *while* they were reading? My professor was right in his expectation of engagement: If you've read something, you should have a thought. How could I get adolescents to buy in?

Later, as I gained experience as a teacher, I saw that many students were like my younger self, afraid to say anything. They wanted to get good grades, but passively—they were too doubtful of their abilities to take charge of their own learning and thinking. Few believed that a purpose of schooling was to develop one's voice (or even knew what it meant to *have* a voice). Of course, I also saw other students who were not necessarily afraid to speak up, but who were completely uninterested in doing work and tried to fake their way through the year. (I've since realized that this could also be a cover for not developing one's genuine voice.) To be sure, there were still other students who were both vocal *and* interested; many of these, however, had trouble coherently formulating their thoughts. As the years progressed, I tried to come up with ways to address all of these situations.

Among the solutions I tried, a system of writing short reading responses—RRs—evolved. This book explains that system. It continues to grow and develop, but the main idea remains the same: *Read, and have a concrete idea about the text to bring to the discussion. You do not have to reveal the meaning of life. You do not have to be "right." You do have to have a thought, one from your own mind, one that is specific, about the reading.* Writing RRs can help all students look more closely at texts and their own thinking, but I've found that there are other benefits that take place over time, below the surface. Students who feel detached from or uninterested in their own learning will start to engage; those who struggle to shape their thoughts will find words. And those who know but are afraid to speak, who get lost in the shuffle of the crowded classroom, will begin to feel the power of their own voices.

Reading, Thinking, Sharing

If you entered my room in my early days as a teacher, you would have seen a very enthusiastic, younger me beaming out energy to a group of twenty-five adolescents. Some of these students were interested, some wanted to make me happy, and some were just being obedient, sitting glassy-eyed and slightly reclined in their chairs. Every now and then I would say something funny and everyone would tune in, but for the most part, the same five students raised their hands. Even though I tried to call on other kids, I mostly called on the eager few. I was passionately trying to help the class understand the basic elements of our text via a comprehension review. Some students understood; some didn't understand but wouldn't ask questions; some didn't care at all but they liked me, or felt sorry for me, or both. Most won't remember the text or its deeper meanings, but they might remember I cared a lot about it, and worked hard.

Now, my classroom looks different. If you visit my sophomore period 3 after the class has read, say, Book VI of the *Iliad* (in which Hector takes a break from battle to run inside the walls of Troy to find his wife, Andromache), you would see students clustered in small groups to share what they have written. As they talk, I pull up a chair and visit.

In the first group, Sondra, a petite, soft-spoken girl, reports, "There's an example of *kleos* [the Greek ideal of glory and fame], and Hector says he wants to be remembered for fighting in this battle, even if it means his wife will be a widow and his son will be an orphan—um. . . ." She pauses as she turns the pages of her text. "That's on page 376." We all go to the page in our own packets. "Well, my Opinion RR is also a feminist critique, that *kleos* is selfish. It seems like a thing men want for themselves, without thinking of anyone else." The term *RR* is code in my class for "reading response," the reading and writing practice my students engage in year-round.

Catherine agrees. Aly excitedly chimes in, "I'm actually reading *Catcher in the Rye* right now, for fun, and I wrote a Connection RR with Book VI. Salinger said, 'The immature man wants to die nobly, but the mature man wants to live humbly.' So the mature man just wants to live and help others, but the immature wants to die and live in the minds of everyone forever. It made me think of Hector." I am thrilled with the connection, but not surprised; students know well that they are expected to bring in associations from outside class.

"I wrote a question," announces Heather, a bright girl with a fluctuating interest in school. "Hector is frantically searching for Andromache in the beginning of the chapter, on page 374. But in other parts of the story, women are just slaves and afterthoughts. Were women really as respected as Andromache? I thought they weren't."

"Hector is different," Catherine declares. "He's special."

"Can you think of any other time when Hector is 'different'?" I ask.

"Well, when he holds up his baby he's different. When he takes his helmet off to make the baby stop crying. That's like a modern-day dad," she explains.

Sondra's spine straightens up suddenly. "It *is* different from the other Greek dads. They don't want their sons to outdo them. Hector prays his son will be *better* than him," she realizes.

Inwardly, I feel victorious. This is a question I would have put on a sheet of important points in the reading—something like "How is Hector different than other father figures in the Greek stories we have read so far?"—but these students have gotten there on their own. I tell them to annotate their new findings, and I move to the next group.

Everyone in the room has a variety of thoughts. Maddie identifies the archetype of the bereft, helpless widow; Cassie questions why Hector and Andromache laughed when their baby screamed (it was because of Hector's horsehair helmet, a fact her group eagerly pointed out). Brendan thinks ancient Greek soldiers are like modern-day soldiers regarding *kleos*, and his group mate Sean agrees, until Phil points out that that the Greeks fought more for a "glorious death" than for a cause, unlike soldiers today. Hannah notices that Homer's epithets for his characters reflect not only the plot of the story, but a bias toward the Greek side. I listen, praise, question, and take notes.

While visiting each group, I can gauge comprehension and identify difficult parts in the text, but the discussions are so much more than a barometer for basic understanding. As groups discuss, they explore each other's thoughts, layering new ideas on to what they wrote for their reading responses. And since their reading responses were created out of personal choice, connection, and prior knowledge, the discussions are rich, interesting events that go far beyond skimming the facts of a piece. The act of discussion becomes like the act of writing when the writer is fully engaged: not merely a reporting of thought, but an extension of it.

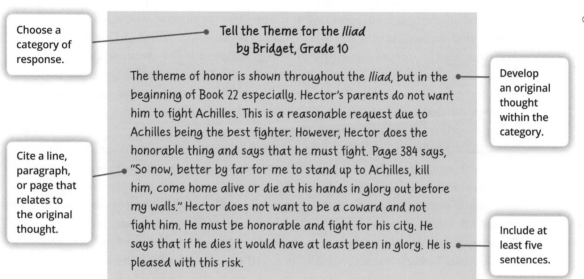

Choose a category of response.

Tell the Theme for the *Iliad*
by Bridget, Grade 10

The theme of honor is shown throughout the *Iliad*, but in the beginning of Book 22 especially. Hector's parents do not want him to fight Achilles. This is a reasonable request due to Achilles being the best fighter. However, Hector does the honorable thing and says that he must fight. Page 384 says, "So now, better by far for me to stand up to Achilles, kill him, come home alive or die at his hands in glory out before my walls." Hector does not want to be a coward and not fight him. He must be honorable and fight for his city. He says that if he dies it would have at least been in glory. He is pleased with this risk.

Develop an original thought within the category.

Cite a line, paragraph, or page that relates to the original thought.

Include at least five sentences.

Figure 1–1 *The Required Parts of a Reading Response*

Reading Responses Versus Comprehension Questions

If you walked into my class now, you would see students who voice their opinions, such as Sondra's estimation of *kleos*. You'd see students who freely ask questions, as Heather did about Andromache, and who make all kinds of connections, such as Aly's tie to *Catcher in the Rye*. You'd see students who examine texts through the eyes of feminism, Marxism, and Queer Theory; who focus on language and craft; and who constantly refer to the text as they discuss. They do these things consistently, organically, and always in variety, based on their own inklings, curiosities, and interests. Through the use of reading responses, each student can—and is expected to—bring his or her real self to the table. It is far from the sterile obedience of comprehension questions.

If I had assigned blanket comprehension questions, the main topics would have been covered—Hector's interior battle between country and family, Andromache's feelings, Hector as a father, and Hector's basic view on fate. Maybe there would have even been a question about modern soldiers and ancient Greek ones. The students would have dutifully answered such a sheet of questions, working together if I let them, perhaps doing a bit of rereading in the process. But the goal would have been much different: Find the Answer. Most students become very skilled at Finding the Answer, since (1) answers are usually tied to grades, and we've taught students to link grades to their basic self-worth, and (2) once the Answer is found, the work is done and no additional thought need be invested. But that's not what happened. Through the sharing of reading responses, instead of Finding the Answer, the goal was to contribute to the discussion.

What's the difference? When your only goal is to contribute to the discussion, you can be wrong. You can ask a "dumb" question. You can give your opinion freely. You can use your life—your outside reading, your knowledge about TV and movies, your family stories. You care about your group mates' thoughts, and not just what the teacher wants. Will you arrive at the Right Answers? Some, for sure. But more importantly, you will meander along the path of deep thinking, the road that leads to evidence-based interpretation rooted in personal experience, prior knowledge, and engagement. The road, perhaps, of personal growth. And isn't that why we all teach in the first place? Who cares if students remember the ancient Greek word for *glory*? But if they remember how the question of fate has been debated by humans since ancient times, if they remember the never-ending struggle between public duty and private love, if they can place themselves, even for a moment, outside the context of their own brief culture—that is the success of learning. If we can get students to be present for their own education, we have succeeded.

Reading with Presence

I call this kind of engagement *reading with presence*: reading with your whole self, your true self, your memories, your opinions, your willingness to learn and grow. It's not just for students. When we approach a text with openness, curiosity, wonder, and the knowledge that we have experiences that shape us while still we seek to evolve, we read with presence. When we allow feelings like confusion, disagreement, or even anger without closing off or looking for the easy resolution, we read with presence. When we feel empathy, when we let the surge of compassion or the ache of sadness or the heart flip of joy flow through us without dismissing it, we read with presence. When we want nothing from a text but what it might have to offer our minds and spirits on its own terms, we read with presence.

And what about texts that are poorly conceived, poorly written, and poorly executed? Texts that are too difficult to understand? Texts that we simply don't care about? The premise still works. Texts are like people: They come into our lives; we may or may not be able to choose them; we may or may not like them in the moment. But we stand in our own self-knowledge and remain open. One must vow to be impractically and doggedly curious. One must cultivate a Buddhist's "beginner's mind" without bias or expectation. As Hamlet said, "The readiness is all." This is what we want to teach our students—how to be lifelong learners, how to be ready learners.

The Courage to Take Risks

This readiness takes a certain level of effort. As in life, one must make an effort to engage, to be present, to accept the uncertainty and complexity of the moment. At the same time, it is possible to overdo it, to become so worried about not missing something that the sense of childlike curiosity is squashed. Imagine a spectrum that ranges from not caring at all to extreme self-consciousness—caring to the point of paralyzing dread over making a mistake. For students at this end of the spectrum, it would be easier to do the automatic thing with little or no awareness involved. In the classroom, these students can devour any worksheet put in front of them; they love the security of getting the right answer. They don't like ambiguity, and they hate the possibility of being wrong in front of each other. This is their greatest classroom fear.

Not only have I witnessed this, students have told me. In the beginning of each year, students complete a survey about participation, and overwhelmingly they say things like, "I would raise my hand more but I don't want to be wrong." I try to combat this with TED talks, articles, and personal stories all about the importance of being wrong. But they will only relax—and they will only take risks—when they truly believe that being wrong is valued. This takes time. When, through the practice of reading responses, these students consistently write their genuine thoughts with their genuine voices, and each time I appreciate their perspective and effort, trust is built.

It's really no different on the other end of the spectrum. In my experience teaching all levels, I believe that all students want to be heard, even if they don't seem to care about English, or school for that matter. All students want to share what they think, and what they already know. Premade comprehension and analysis questions won't necessarily make space for that, but reading responses will. Assuring reluctant learners that there are no "right answers" when writing RRs takes the pressure off. When they realize that they can get full credit, and my full attention, for simply writing what they think, they eventually start to contribute. When they realize that I truly appreciate the prior knowledge they bring into the room, they begin to talk and write more about it.

Caleb, a student who often engaged in class but was reluctant to do any written work, fell into this category. He was in the small group of students in our school who attended the local vocational school for a half day; he was from the rural side of our district, which also makes up a smaller population in our school. He had friends and seemed to get along with everyone, but was not in the mainstream group that worried about grades. For several weeks, he did not write reading responses at all and when I would pass by his desk to check, I would repeat the directions and encourage him to try. "OK," he would answer, every time.

Then one day, he had two reading responses written. We had been reading "The Fisherman and the Jinnee" from *One Thousand and One Nights*. "These are probably wrong," he said, "but I wrote a connection about how the fisherman in the story pulled in garbage and useless stuff on his first four casts and I can relate to that. And then I wrote a character trait about how it said he went fishing every day to feed his family, so that shows he's a good family man because he cares about them."

I was ecstatic, but I also did not want to overreact in front of the class. As I examined his writing, I could tell he had met all the requirements of writing the responses. "That's not wrong at all, Caleb! That's it. You did it—you have your own thoughts, you included quotes from the story, you labeled your categories, you wrote five sentences—that's it. Now tell me more about how fishing today compares to fishing in the story." And we talked for a couple minutes. For weeks after, Caleb brought up the characters and themes from this story as comparison springboards for other stories.

Does this mean that Caleb—and other reluctant learners—magically transformed into a motivated, meticulous student? Not necessarily. But when I conference with these students, and we discuss what they have written, they get my full presence. I ask questions about their opinions; I am impressed with their connections; I commend their questions and encourage them to ask more. I connect with them as learners and human beings, and, little by little, they start to care. Some will make dramatic transformations; others will remain guarded, but will have engaged more than they ever had before.

Starting with What Students Have in Their Minds

On a midyear survey, James, a student who was motivated and high achieving but hesitant to raise his hand in whole-group discussions, remarked, "This is the first English class that I have taken that gave me the opportunities to write what came to my mind, even if some people consider it unimportant and meaningless." When I read that, I marveled that this sixteen-year-old had made it through ten years of schooling carrying the notion that "some people" think his thoughts are unimportant and meaningless. When did that start, I wondered, and why had it persisted? I also wondered how many other students felt the same way. How many of them felt their own thoughts were just noise, and the Right Answers were to be found elsewhere, from a teacher or the certified "smart" kid in class? As teachers, our business is in helping students express, refine, and deepen their own thinking—not in simply broadcasting the right answers. We must start with whatever they bring us in their minds.

The "readiness" mentioned above pertains to us too. We must be willing to step into the often messy ambiguity of student thinking. At the same time, we must resist doing the thinking for them. We must acknowledge and appreciate where they are, as we give them the most appropriate tools at the most opportune moments to improve. We must be present to them as people and as learners, and present to their past experiences and their thoughts, however jumbled or profound or reluctant they may be.

Responsible Reading

The idea of students organically responding to literature is certainly not new: Indeed it stems from Rosenblatt's (2005) Reader Response Theory, or as she preferred to call it, the Transactional Theory of Reading and Writing. As Rosenblatt (2005) states, "Books do not simply happen to people. People also happen to books" (62). Educators have known this for some time but still struggle for meaningful, manageable ways to get students engaged in reading and to push them to think deeply about texts. On one hand, teachers want students to connect with text not only intellectually but also personally and to see the text as relevant to their life and experience. On the other, we don't want students to espouse an "anything goes" stance to approaching a text, thinking that they can attach any random meaning to the words; we want them to remain rooted in the text itself as they personally engage with it. Rosenblatt (2005) calls this "responsible reading":

> Although there isn't a single "correct" interpretation of any text for all circumstances, that doesn't necessarily rule out responsible reading. We can consider some interpretations better or poorer than others. Or we can find that readers bringing different knowledge and assumptions or in different social and historical contexts may have equally defensible interpretations. (xxiv)

At one point in the classroom conversation at the start of this chapter, Robert declared to his group that Hector was a horrible person for laughing when his baby cried; in Robert's view, Hector didn't care about the baby and enjoyed watching him suffer. He cited the line of the laughing. Robert's small group quickly pounced, explaining to him that Hector laughed in a fatherly way and had hastily removed the cause of the problem (his scary helmet). They reread the lines that supported their interpretation. "Ohhh," Robert said, "Now I get it. It was a 'That's so cute' laugh." Through the discussion, Robert's group led him to responsible reading.

English teachers must work to consistently balance the desire to create a "live circuit" of interaction with text and the desire to create responsible readers that habitually, doggedly even, refer to the text as they give their opinions and analyses (Rosenblatt 2005, 64). Again, comprehension questions are not the answer: Viewing reading skills as solely objective and neutral, as done when employing comprehension questions, ignores the creative capacities of the reader; the generative activity of reading becomes oversimplified, and the identities of readers dissolve in uniformity (Sulzer 2014). One student, Halle, put it this way: "RRs are a great way to express oneself without giving a boring answer . . . [they] allow the writer to connect the texts not only to themselves, but to other things that they are passionate about." Students want to find personal relevance in what they're learning. As educators search for more effective ways to get students to understand and respond to texts, the techniques that rise to the top involve personal engagement (Alexander 2012). That's where reading responses come in.

Sharing Reading Responses

As can be seen from the discussions above, once students have written an RR or two about a text, they have something to say in class. It may be a minor point, or it may be a major point, but it is a concrete thought and it is tied to a specific part of the text. Most students will be eager to share their RRs, elaborating as they do; reluctant contributors can be simply asked to read what they have written. No longer can a student say, "I don't know" when asked to react to a reading. If questioned on the spot immediately following a reading, students may genuinely not know what to say. But when given time to write, and a list of choices to scaffold their reactions, all students can come up with something.

Discussion is the necessary culmination of RR writing. Letting students come up with the points of a text that they think are significant or interesting can at first feel disconcerting; in the beginning, I wondered if they would cover all the aspects of the text which I believed were important. Fisher, Frye, and Lapp (2012) explain that many teachers may be hesitant or find it difficult to release their traditional role and let students lead the discussion. However, teachers who espouse discussion have two core beliefs: first, that students "have something worthwhile to say," which may differ from the teacher's views, and second, that teachers will have to give up some of the control of knowledge (15). This is so hard for us because we have been trained to "pass on" knowledge in some kind of mythical, pristine form, and in some kind of mythical, pristine transaction. We want desperately for students to succeed and to embrace the joys of lifelong reading, and at times it can feel easier and more effective to simply tell them what they should know. But real learning is messier, harder won, and more genuine.

I quickly realized that letting students lead the discussion, whether in small groups or the whole class, using their RRs not only covers everything but is exponentially more productive and interesting. During discussion, RRs serve as barometers of comprehension and prior knowledge. Students will often admit difficulties in understanding if they wrote an RR focused on a question, prompting their classmates to offer clarification. A student may bring up a question that several others wrote about as well, or one that many students had but did not write about. This opens a viable teachable moment, one that may have been lost if I was merely lecturing or reviewing a list of questions. When students incorporate prior knowledge into their RRs, especially if they choose the Connection category, it always livens discussion and jogs the collective memories of the class. Connection RRs engage the students on their own level, tapping into generational experiences in a way that a teacher, working alone, never could.

Discussing RRs gives students the added benefit of using literary terms in a natural way. When students present their RRs to their small group, they must give the RR category, cite a part of the text, and explain their thinking. In doing this, they apply literary terms to their own interpretations. Frey and Fisher (2013) explain that "accessing complex texts requires collaborative conversations . . . students need practice with academic language if they are to become proficient in that language" (74–75).

I see this practice happen all the time in class. For example, I will overhear a student say something like, "I wrote about the villain—the, the—what is it again? Antisomething?" And another member of the group will say, "Antagonist." Discussing the text with the framework of RRs gives students the structure of academic language in an accessible way. Prior to the previous discussion about the *Iliad*, I had used terms like *epithet* and *kleos* for several days; listening to students use those terms on their own—tripping over both the meanings and the pronunciations—reminded me that it was new for them, and they needed the practice trying the words out in their own conversations. It's the difference between watching a video on free throws and actually shooting the ball.

Discussion brings the act of reading and writing full circle; it both completes and extends the process. Students read and respond to the best of their ability, each from his or her limited but personally informed perspective. Then, they engage with each other, voicing their own thoughts and listening to others. They explain, defend, and refine their ideas; they collaborate and go deeper. And when a group puts their heads together, they not only gain a fuller understanding of the text; they become stronger readers and thinkers than when they began.

The Parts of a Reading Response

"Can we just do normal questions like in other years?" Aidan asked. "Writing RRs is *hard*. It's too much thinking."

"Really?" I countered. "Thinking up your own thoughts is 'hard'? They're *your* thoughts. Is it really that hard to think them?"

Aidan laughed a self-deprecating chuckle. "No, no. I get it. Sometimes it's just hard starting from scratch, you know?"

I do know, both from my own experience and from listening to students. I get Aidan's question often, and that fact confirms, for me, the need to push students to do the work of writing RRs. In a world full of "retweets" and "likes," it is easy to skim along the surface of things without genuine reflection, deep deliberation, or original thought of any kind. It is work to think, and as teachers, we must drive students to do it.

If the prospect of writing "from scratch" feels daunting for many students, most settle into a routine and become comfortable with the method and the constant demand for writing. Aidan himself wrote a beautiful collection of RRs by the end of the year. Of course, an RR practice is not writing completely from scratch—it contains scaffolds to help students face the blank page in a meaningful way. In this chapter, we'll explore how the RR scaffolds help students embark on a yearlong journey of literary criticism and intellectual growth, filling notebooks with responses that are both personal and scholarly.

The directions for writing a meaningful RR are direct and applicable to any text. In response to their reading, students must do the following:

- Choose a category of response, using the list of possible categories, and write the category name at the top of the response.

- Develop an original thought within that category and write out the thought.

- Find, copy, and cite a line, paragraph, or page from the text that relates to the original thought.

- Keep writing and thinking for at least five sentences.

Choose a Category

At some point in their reading, students must scan through the RR categories and choose one for their response. Although dozens of possible categories exist, I recommend giving students a list of 10–15 from which to choose. This list can change or broaden at the end of a quarter or semester, but it is important not to overwhelm students with choices, especially in the beginning. Figure 2–1 is a sample RR instruction sheet with fifteen categories; this is the one I give my own students at the beginning of the first semester.

During the second quarter, once students are adept at the practice, I give them a sheet of additional categories. Notice that each category includes some questions or prompts to help students generate a thought about their responses. The simple act of noticing one's own thinking and browsing a list of ways to think about texts will help students stock their toolbox of what good readers notice.

Part 2 of this book details more than thirty possible categories, but that list of categories is certainly not exhaustive; each year new categories crop up in my classroom and I incorporate them into our pool of possibilities. One year, for example, a student diverged from the Connection category and titled his response, "What would Mr. Lavelle say?" (Mr. Lavelle is a Spanish teacher at our school.) I thought this idea—imagining the voice of a respected other—deserved to be its own category; it now appears on my second-semester list. Another student once titled a response "Finding an Archetype" and explained, "I was going to write a Character Trait RR about how this character is an archetype and I thought that it was more than just a trait. So I gave it my own category." From that point, I happily included Archetype Alert into our list of choices. The majority of the time, students use the categories

Reading Responses (RRs)
Put this paper in the front of your notebook!!

Directions: As you read, annotate or put a Post-it next to any line, sentence, or section that jumps out at you. Write a brief note to yourself so you can remember what you were thinking. If nothing jumps out at you by the time you have finished reading, go back and find something to respond to.

Write out the RR fully on paper. **YOU MUST**:

- Label which **type** of RR category you are using (see below).
- Use an **original thought** in your response; don't just summarize.
- Quote a sentence or phrase from the text that supports your thinking, and give the **page number**, **paragraph**, or **line number** of the quote.
- Write **at least five complete sentences**.

Types of RRs

1. **Give an Opinion:** Tell what you think or feel about a certain part, and why. You could react to an aspect of character, plot, theme, language, tone, style—anything in the text. But you must be specific.

2. **Ask a Question:** Write a specific question. This can be a question about something you don't understand in the text, or a larger question (about life, literature, or anything) that the text made you consider. Remember, you must still write five sentences—you can do this by explaining what you understand so far before asking the question, or by trying to answer your question after you ask it.

3. **Make a Connection:** A certain point in the text reminds you of another story, poem, movie, song, or something in real life. How are the two alike? Be specific.

4. **Character Description:** You notice a detail about a character (what he or she looks like, thinks, says, or does). Why is it important? What trait or other idea does it reveal about that character?

5. **Spot the Setting:** You notice a part that refers to the place or time of the story or poem. Why is it important? How does it relate to the theme, characters, or plot?

6. **Mark the Motivation:** You realize a character's motive(s)—what a character wants. Explain what the motives are and how they affect the story or other characters. Why are these motives important?

7. **Detect a Conflict:** You sense a conflict in the story—it can be large or small, external or internal. Describe it, and explain why it is important in the story.

8. **Find Foreshadowing:** You read something that seems like a hint to what will come later. Explain why you think this, and make a prediction.

9. **Clarify the Climax:** You read a part that you realize is the biggest event (or most important moment) in the story. Explain why it is so important and what questions or problems get resolved because of it.

10. **See the Significance:** You realize a certain part in the text is important; you spot a significant passage. Why do you think it's important? What does it mean? What does it tell you about the entire book, story, or poem?

Figure 2–1 *Sample RR Instruction Sheet*   *(continues)*

Figure 2-1 *Sample RR Instruction Sheet (continued)*

11. **Theme Recognition:** You find a sentence or two that might connect to a theme (the message or "So what?") of the piece. Tell the theme, and explain how that portion of text relates to it.

12. **Cite the Claim:** You find a sentence or passage you think is the author's main thesis or claim. Explain why you think it is the central claim of the piece.

13. **Language Recognition:** You notice some engaging sensory details, a simile or metaphor, some onomatopoeia or alliteration, some parallelism, an interesting epithet, or something else. Maybe you notice a single word and wonder about why the author chose it. Whatever you notice, quote it, and explain how it adds to the text. Does it contribute to the mood or characterization? Does it relate to a theme? Could it have a deeper meaning? What would that be?

14. **Interesting Intro:** You think the author's introduction is interesting, clever, or engaging. Tell what the author did to make it so interesting and why you think that is effective.

15. **Clever Conclusion:** You think the author's conclusion or clincher is really effective. Tell what technique the author used and why it works.

supplied on the sheet. But once students are familiar with the process, they naturally create their own categories if they have a thought that doesn't seem to fit in an existing category. I am always delighted by this and encourage it; it reveals engagement, creativity, and close analysis.

Sometimes, students will create categories that I don't add to our master list, but I encourage nonetheless. Recently a student shared an RR categorized as Themes Across Texts, in which she discussed the same theme explored in two separate works. In my mind, this qualifies as a simple Connection, but I applauded the student's effort to be as specific as possible. These occasional creative forays into category design remind me how much the act of reading, and thinking about reading, is a generative and active process.

The Importance of Choice

In the process of writing RRs, the importance of choice cannot be understated. Students feel like they are in control of their responses; they can view the text through whatever lens they choose. Much research has demonstrated that choice positively affects intrinsic motivation, effort, performance, and competence (Patall, Cooper, and Robinson 2008). In addition, when students are given choices regarding homework (as RRs often are), they not only feel more motivated and competent, they perform better on tests and complete homework more often (Patall, Cooper, and Wynn 2010). With choice and self-expression, students become more engaged in their work and willing to participate (Fisher, Frye, and Lapp 2012).

Genre Flexibility

RRs can be used with any genre, fiction or nonfiction. I do not specify which ones students should choose with any specific genre. Although most of the RR categories are not genre-specific, many of them, such as Character Trait or Cite the Claim, were formulated with a genre in mind. Even so, students will mix categories and genres in creative ways. For example, they will write a Clever Conclusion RR (one I formulated for nonfiction prose) to elucidate the technique an author used to end a story or poem. Students have applied the Spot the Setting RR to newspaper articles; they have chosen the Cite the Claim for a sonnet. Whenever this happens, I commend the student for thinking flexibly and creatively.

By letting students choose how to respond to a text, teachers compel them to pay closer attention to what they are reading and to become absorbed in the text as a whole. When students have prewritten questions, they read on Rosenblatt's (2005) efferent end of the continuum, seeking only the information that will answer the question and end the exercise. This is what we teach students to do for standardized tests: read searching for answers, with the questions in mind. The goal is not to enjoy or be transported by the reading; the goal is to answer the question. By giving students a choice about how to respond, however, we decrease answer-seeking, efferent reading and push students toward the aesthetic end of Rosenblatt's (2005) continuum, where they become more complete readers, focusing on "what was being lived through during the reading, on the ideas as they are embodied in the images, the sensations, the feelings, the changing moods" (xxvii).

Of course, the efferent and aesthetic stances are not inherently good or bad, but Rosenblatt (2005) feels that as students age, less and less classroom emphasis is placed on aesthetic reading, which she views as a loss: "Reading, especially aesthetic reading, extends the scope of that environment and feeds the growth of the individual, who can then bring a richer self to further transactions with life and literature" (81). With the practice of RR writing, students do not have to answer specific questions with definitive answers. Instead, they can read with presence, and decide at the end what aspect they would like to respond to.

The Need for Direction

Although choice is a vital component to engagement and learning, some direction will always benefit students. Asking students to respond to a text in any way they choose, without any guidance about the possibilities, could actually leave them bored and confused in the end. Usually, when given a completely open-ended response option, students will give shallow opinions about a text—they will claim that they liked it or didn't like it and offer a few surface reasons why. Without being taught how to think more deeply about a text, this superficial analysis will quickly get old. Students may begin to sense that they are missing the nuances and deeper meanings the text potentially holds. One student, Nichole, expressed the frustration of not being able to effectively say what she was thinking before learning how to write RRs: "I'm starting to get a feel for expressing my thoughts," she said, "instead of keeping everything bottled up inside my mind," without knowing how to express it. She had thoughts about texts; she just didn't know how to get at them. Later in the year, she felt her writing "flowed" more—she was able to find doorways into her own thinking.

The RR categories, given to students in the beginning of the year, are meant to be a vehicle to help them think more clearly and deeply about a text. They are the scalpels students can use to dissect the text; without them, students are fumbling with the blunt instruments of their own guesswork, and whatever prior knowledge they may have, on the exterior of the text. "I'm seeing a lot of opposites in this poem," Meghan said about Number 22 of the *Tao te Ching*. "But what kind of RR would that be?" I told her that it depended how she wanted to examine the lines—as a language technique? As a theme? Or, did they remind her of something else? Did she have an opinion about their meaning? She thought for a minute. "It's definitely making a point—it's the theme of the poem, I think. I'll write about that." She skimmed the RR categories. "Theme Recognition," she said.

When reading through the RR categories in search of something to write, students will consider the text in new ways, from each angle on the list; this alone will make them think more critically about the text. When actually crafting an RR, students must take their initial understanding and develop it more deeply to reach the five-sentence minimum.

This combination of choice and direction strikes the balance between what Gallagher (2009) describes as the overteaching and underteaching of books: "Overteaching books . . . prevents students from achieving reading flow," but at the same time, educators should give students "the proper level of instructional support without abandoning them or without drowning them in a sea of sticky-notes, double-entry journals, and worksheets" (87). Giving students RR categories and asking them to choose a way to respond to the text encourages growth while preventing a sense of being overwhelmed.

The Meaningfulness of Metacognition

By labeling each RR, the student must engage in a basic level of metacognition: He is not only responding to the text, but thinking about *how* he is responding. Research has shown that metacognitive knowledge and control contribute to stronger skills in reading comprehension (Carretti et al. 2013) and critical thinking (Magno 2010).

When students label an RR, I rarely "correct" them. If the label seems not to apply to the actual RR at all, I would question the student about her thought process. If she can make a logical case for the label, I'm satisfied—it's the act of metacognition that I'm after, not right or wrong label. For example, one of my students, Maddie, thought that a character's unreasonableness qualified for a Find the Foreshadowing RR and not a Character Trait RR. I asked her why she chose that label. "The hawk"—the character in question, from the short story "Sibi" in the *Mahabharata*— "is over-the-top demanding. It gives you a sense of what's going to happen," she said. I asked her if that didn't instead sound like a trait. "It could be a trait, but I think it's so extreme that when you read it you know something bad is going to come out of it. He keeps pushing the king, and you know that will lead to some major incident. That's what I wrote about." Sure enough, she had explained that thought in detail in her RR. Case made.

As stated earlier, I also don't discourage students from inventing categories if they feel they cannot find the one they want on the handout. Abby, a bright student who loves poetry, wrote an RR called "Life Lesson" when responding to the ancient Chinese poem "Thick Grow the Rush Leaves." I asked her how a life lesson was different from a theme. "I feel like a theme is just one word, pertaining only to that story," she said, "whereas a life lesson is more general and can apply to anyone." I pushed her a bit more to explain. She said that the poem in question, about a girl longing to see her love but who cannot find him, could teach the reader that "you have to give people space." But the theme of the poem, to Abby, was simply "loss." "The life lesson is bigger," she argued. I was intrigued, but satisfied: She made a logical case for her choice, and metacognition was achieved. For myself, I reflected on how students are taught the concept of theme, and wondered how, or if, it should be expanded so that students more readily would incorporate this sense of a life lesson into their understanding.

Sometimes, especially in the beginning, students will forget to include a label. When I conference with them, they often begin the way my student Joe did in responding to African Proverbs, by saying, "I wrote about how I agree with the proverb 'You cannot chase two gazelles'" instead of "I wrote an opinion about how I agree with the proverb." I let Joe explain his thoughts completely, and then said, "You're making an interesting and valid point here, but you forgot to label the RR—what do you think it would be?" I gave him time to think and consult his RR list. When he hesitated, I pointed out actual words he used in his response: "You have words like *feel* and *agree* here—what do you think?" He quickly realized it was an Opinion RR, and wrote the category above his response.

Occasionally, a student will leave the category label blank not because of forgetfulness or carelessness, but because she genuinely didn't know what to write. This becomes a very teachable moment. When Emily left her RR for "The River-Merchant's Wife: A Letter" unlabeled, I first asked her if she forgot. "No," she said, "I just really didn't know what to put." The response was about how she liked that the poem was a story and not "telling you what to do" like some other aphoristic texts we had been reading. She wanted to label it with something more specific than simply Give an Opinion. "It sounds to me like you're alluding to something about the form," I suggested, and we discussed the differences between aphoristic poetry and ballads. In the end, she decided it fell under the Joy of Genre category.

Use an Original Thought

The next step is to write out the response, including some bit of original thinking. By "original thinking" I mean *some thought that is not in the text*. It is the cornerstone to this technique. The thought can be small, but it must exist. Making connections, making inferences, or giving evaluations all count as original thought. For example, saying Gilgamesh is altruistic is an inference and therefore an original thought, just like connecting a Greek myth to a Native American story. Comparing the love triangle from King Arthur to the one in *The Walking Dead* is an original thought. Noticing the parallelism in a Rumi poem is not an original thought by itself, but speculating on its effect—to make the poem feel like a song, for example, or to emphasize the theme—is. I ask students again and again, "What do you want to *say* about what you see in the text?" to nudge them into the realm of original thought.

Beyond Summarizing

When beginning the practice of RRs, students often merely summarize what they've read. Although summarizing is an important skill inherent in any RR category, it is not enough by itself. For example, for a response about setting, if students only needed to list and cite a setting, such as the desert or a boat, this practice would be no different than answering a basic question. But in the Spot the Setting category, students are asked to think about *why* the setting is important. Now, the response deepens: Students must not only recognize the desert but also ask themselves why the desert is the perfect place to hold this portion of the plot. They could ask themselves if the desert is symbolic or tied to the theme. The guiding questions on the instruction sheet are designed to help students arrive at an original thought and push past mere identification. For this reason, students should keep the instructions sheet beside them as they write.

When I discuss students' RRs with them, I point out the difference between plain summaries and summaries with an original thought. Many RRs can't be written at all without an original thought (such as the Give an Opinion, Make a Connection, and What Would _____ Say? categories). But often, students will simply identify something in the text without further analysis, such as an introductory technique without telling why it's effective or a claim without telling how it relates to the rest of the text. When we read King Arthur, for example, plot summaries crop up often as RRs because the story is so dense with action. Arthur journeys, fights, hosts, decides, quests—and it's easy for students to merely report all this. I'll ask them questions specific to the moment they've written about, such as *What does Arthur's decision here reveal about him as a person?* or *How does this particular quest point to a theme of the story?* By nudging students to add an original thought to their summaries, we can help them better engage with the text. In addition, this skill is the core of longer academic essays: All theses are, in fact, single original thoughts. The rest of the paper is comprised of paragraphs and pages mounted to prove that one thought. RRs are a microcosm of that process.

If needed, I will conduct a whole-class minilesson demonstrating the difference between pure summary and summary with an original thought. It's interesting to notice that students have been so well trained in summarizing—an important skill— but feel unsure about having their own thoughts about a text. We've taught them to identify, classify, support, and summarize. We haven't necessarily taught them to think for themselves. Original thought takes effort, and I cheerlead it all year long.

Original Thoughts Are Automatically Differentiated

When writing an RR, students respond at the level, and from the angle, they are able. In doing so, students self-differentiate. Teachers don't have to generate extra materials or divide students into groups; differentiation happens naturally when constructing RRs. With a choice of ten to fifteen possible ways to respond, every student can find something to write about. When asked what she thinks about a text, no student should ever say, "I don't know," even if she did not understand the majority of it. She might not comprehend the innermost meaning of the text's symbolism or the intricacies of its figurative language, but she can point out a character trait, explain an important setting, or make a connection to another story, all with a specific bit of evidence.

One student, Julia, enjoyed writing RRs in the Language Recognition category. She was quick to spot similes and personification, and she could effectively speculate about their deeper meaning or purpose. She told me that she often wrote about figurative language when she didn't fully understand what was going on in the story. In class discussions, she would clarify any confusion she had with plot and theme, but at least she wasn't sitting there empty-handed. She knew her contribution about figurative language would still be valuable.

Even within the RR categories, differentiation is possible: For the Language Recognition category, for example, one student may focus on a simile whose symbolism is apparent, and another may explain the effect of the assonance upon the mood of the entire piece. Both responses would count. And during the classroom discussion, students will educate each other. Connections are often where I see the most variety. When we read the sayings of Confucius, for example, the same aphorism can be processed in a myriad of ways: One student may make a connection to contemporary American culture, another may cite an example from Buck's *The Good Earth*, and another might quote one of Ben Franklin's proverbs. The RRs would vary in depth, prior knowledge, and wording. But all would be relevant and make for a rich discussion.

Cite the Text

Students must ground their original thoughts by citing the text. They should quote a sentence or phrase and give a line number, paragraph number, or page number. By tying their thought, observation, question, or opinion to a specific spot in the text, students create the foundation on which their original idea can stand. They practice the first step in "responsible reading" by pointing to a place in the text that, in their minds, supports their thinking. This does not mean that their thinking is automatically correct, but it means their idea is at least rooted in the text.

Using Citations During Discussion

With a citation, students immediately have a reference point to use during discussion. When a student reads or explains her RR in a small or large group, everyone should consult the cited sentence or phrase in their own copies, and reread as they listen. Thus, the listeners also journey through the thought process of the reader's mind. Again, responsible reading is at play: With the exact passage before them, a group can better absorb or question the reader's analysis. Students can point to sentences before or after the cited portion; they can tie the cited part to sections of text further away. If a student had not previously noted the passage, he could add to his annotations as the RR writer talks; if he had made notes, he could compare his thinking with his classmates'. Or, through discussion, students could arrive at a new understanding of the lines. Whatever the outcome, with a specific piece of text to focus on, students are not merely listening to the airy speculations or nebulous generalizations of a peer; they are working with the author's actual words, and in doing so, interacting with the text all over again.

Close Reading Correlation

Writing RRs is first and foremost an exercise in close reading. Frey and Fisher (2013) define close reading as reading "for a level of detail not typically sought after in everyday reading" (45). They advocate that students stay anchored in the text "to develop a fairly sophisticated understanding of what the author actually said" (45). To create an RR, in any category and in any genre, a student must pinpoint a line, paragraph, or stanza and dig a bit deeper into that selection of text. Writing RRs requires students to choose a spot in a text to examine more closely. They may do this during reading or after reading, depending on how they formulate their RR. But at some point, they must close read.

I usually assign two RRs at a time with a one-sitting chunk of either assigned or independent reading. For example, I might have students read the first half of Book IV of the *Iliad* and write two RRs. Or, I might assign two short poems and instruct students to write one RR for each. With independent reading, students decide when and where in the text they will write their RRs, and they keep a section of their notebooks for this purpose. I often assign these as homework, but RRs can be done in class as well. On the surface, it may seem like students are only focusing on one or two parts of the text closely and not adequately working to process the whole reading. But this is not the case. If students write their RRs as a postreading exercise, the initial act of merely choosing an RR category compels them to consider the text from several angles in search of one that could work at that moment. And after selecting a category, students usually reread the applicable portion of text several times, formulating an original thought.

Even if students have an idea for an RR while they are reading, and they have a category selected without considering the list of categories, they are still working toward a deeper understanding of the overall text. First, they are reading with presence, paying attention to their own thoughts as they read. And second, zooming in on a small moment helps illuminate larger swaths of text. Gallagher (2009) call this a "Big Chunk/Little Chunk Philosophy": "If students aren't directed to read small chunks of text closely, they will never learn to reach deeper levels of analysis" (9). When each student comes to the discussion with his or her small, closely read bit of text, they can stitch together their patches of insight into a fuller quilt of understanding.

Write Five Sentences

Five sentences is a minimum, and this length can be adjusted up or down, depending on class or student level. We write not only to record thought, but to extend thought;

often we don't know what we fully think until we begin writing about it. By forcing themselves to add two or three sentences to their basic first thought, students may stumble upon a deeper, more nuanced understanding of what they were initially thinking. As playwright Edward Albee says, "I write to find out what I'm thinking about" (Murray 1990, 4). Flannery O'Connor agrees: "I write because I don't know what I think until I read what I say" (Murray 1990, 8). Sure, the writer has a surface topic in mind when she sits down to write, but it is during the act of writing that new, unrealized thoughts are revealed.

Students tell me all the time that an RR changes as they write. Sometimes they begin writing with a question, and by the end of the RR, they've answered their own question. Or, the thought evolves into something deeper: When reading T'ao Ch'ien's "Form, Shadow, Spirit," a poem in three voices, Madison explained that she began writing a response about tone, because each voice had a distinct quality. "But as I wrote," she said, "I realized that each voice had its own message about life, so the RR became about theme." On the top of her response she had crossed out *Tell the Tone* and written *Tone Leading to Theme*.

This experience of learning *through* writing is a well-known phenomenon among regular writers; no student should leave English class without conviction of its existence. Author and poet Jane Yolen (2007) advises writers to "be prepared for serendipity." She says, "Be prepared as you write to be surprised by your own writing." If students read a text and only annotate it, they will not reap the richer benefits that come with having written about it.

By going further, students will write themselves into deeper comprehension and analysis. Since they have to "get" to five sentences, students must keep thinking, find more evidence from the text, or both. O'Reilley (1998) declares that "writing exercises . . . can create a spacious moment" (6). By having students write regularly, we help them to create a space for their thoughts to grow.

Meaningful, Consistent, Low-Stakes Writing Practice

When students write RRs several times a week, they develop a habit of deliberate writing. This habit leads to writing fluency—a certain level of comfort with writing about texts and with writing in general. As noted previously, crafting RRs is more directed than freewriting. However, it is just as low stakes: Students' grades won't plummet for wrong ideas or grammatical errors.

Checking RRs

When I check RRs, I use "detailed completion" criteria: I am checking for completion as opposed to judging the rightness or wrongness of the answer, but I am checking for specific markers that indicate thought and effort. I usually count an RR for four points: one for length, one for having a category, one for having a cited quote, and one for having an original thought. Recently, I've thrown a fifth point in there, one I call "best work." Sometimes a student will have all the criteria, but the sentences will be extremely short or have remnants from lunch period on them, or the thinking seems easy compared with the student's prior work, or the cited quote is from the first paragraph of the reading and as I question the student, it becomes clear that she didn't read the entire passage. "Is this your best work?" I'll ask them. They'll usually admit if it's not.

The detailed completion grading method holds students accountable for the effort, but allows them to take risks in their thinking. Students never lose points for the rightness of their original thought or for having the correct category labeled. Nor do they lose points for grammar or spelling, though I will tap into a teachable moment in those areas if it arises. Gallagher (2016) tweeted that "exploration, risk, and failure are essential components in a writer's growth. Exploration and risk will not occur if everything is graded," and I've tried to incorporate that belief in my day-to-day checking of reading responses, by ensuring students they will never be wrong with RRs. The end result is a regular practice of structured but exploratory writing.

This regular writing practice will activate the "individual linguistic reservoir" and make the student a more articulate writer in general (Rosenblatt 2005, 17). Gallagher (2011) believes that "students are not being given enough time to 'deliberately' practice their writing," and therefore are unable to become experts at it

(233). He cites a study by Ericsson, Prietula, and Cokely (2007), which found that to become adept at anything, people must deliberately and consistently practice tasks that are just outside of one's abilities; one must also learn to monitor and teach oneself—an opportunity not often provided in schools. Although students must obviously be given extended time to write longer pieces, they can develop valuable skills and fluency through the daily challenge of writing RRs. William Zinsser (2006), in his classic work, *On Writing Well*, states it best: "You learn to write by writing . . . The only way to learn to write is to force yourself to produce a certain number of words on a daily basis" (59). Jane Yolen (2016) recommends: "Exercise the writing muscle every day, even if it is only a letter, notes, a title list, a character sketch, a journal entry. Writers are like dancers, like athletes. Without that exercise, the muscles seize up." Anyone who has written regularly knows this is true.

In their RR Analysis Papers (explained fully in Chapter 4), students often reflect on how their writing has changed, and for every student the change is different. One student, Matt, felt his endurance for writing grow stronger. After a couple months, he said, "My RRs have grown in length and content. In the beginning, I felt myself struggling to meet the five-sentence minimum, but over time, I've found it much easier to write them." Another student, Ari, found just the opposite: "Over the course of the semester, my reading responses have become shorter. However, they have become more focused and more to the point. I could write in six sentences what would have taken me a page to convey. They are becoming more about quality and less about quantity."

Cassie felt the same way. At the beginning of the year she wrote extremely long RRs, sometimes covering an entire page. Over the course of a semester, though, they became more concise. She explained that even though her responses got shorter, they also got better. "In the beginning of the year I just summarized the stories or parts I was talking about. But now I feel as though I am actually analyzing the material and thinking more in depth," she wrote. With consistent practice, she was able to recognize and improve the complexity of her own thinking. Another student, Antonia, reflected not on length but on the quality of her sentences: "At the beginning of the year," she said, "I had many small, and rather choppy, sentences. However, over the year, I have begun to slowly blend my thoughts into fewer, longer sentences." I had not graded these students in writing style when reading their RRs—these are changes that occurred naturally from the act of writing often on a regular basis.

Different Processes for Writing RRs

Students enter the process of writing an RR in different ways, and they rarely use the exact same process every time. Students quickly internalize the RR process and develop the habits they prefer. Some possibilities:

✧ A student finishes an entire reading, has an original thought she wants to write about, finds the appropriate category, finds a line to quote, and writes.

✧ A student finishes an entire reading, does not have an idea for an RR, consults the categories list, reads through it until a thought occurs to him, finds a line to match the thought, and writes.

✧ A student is reading and a possible RR thought jumps into her head, such as "Wow, this character is arrogant," or "That was an unexpected surprise!" She scribbles a note in the margin. After reading, she returns to the spot, finds an appropriate corresponding category, and writes.

✧ A student has an original thought while reading and decides to stop, find a category that fits, and write the whole RR then and there. When finished, he goes back to his reading.

✧ A student approaches reading intending to write in a certain category, for example, "I really like thinking of the main character; I'm going to write a Character Trait RR about him," or "I haven't written a Language Recognition RR yet; that's what I will try now." She looks for a line to cite as she reads. She may write the RR when she finds the line, or she may note the line and then write when finished reading.

✧ A student completes the reading and begins writing about a certain topic, moment, or point he has in mind. He finds a quote, uses it, and writes at least five sentences. Then he asks himself, "What category is this?" and rereads what he has written. He searches for an appropriate category, tweaks his response if needed, and labels the response.

In the beginning of the year, I hand out the sheet of the RR directions and the fifteen initial categories. I introduce the process by saying something like this:

Here is a practice we will be working on all year—it's called reading responses, *or RRs* for short. An RR is a short paragraph about what we've read. When you write them, you can write about any part of the text that stands out for you. So that means there are no wrong answers. It's just you, thinking, and then writing about what you're thinking. You'll get used to this format pretty quickly, and soon you'll be able to look at any reading and have a solid, interesting thought about it. Most students really enjoy the freedom of being able to write what they want about the reading. Let me repeat myself—you can't get it wrong. I want to know what your genuine thoughts are about our readings, and as long as you're trying to put your thoughts into words, as long as you're making the effort, you'll succeed. There are a few guidelines, though, and that's what we'll practice today. Let's look at the sheet and practice one or two.*

From there, I explain the rules and briefly go over the categories. Because guiding questions accompany each one, I don't "teach" each category. Most, if not all, of the categories, at least in this first list, are usually familiar to the students by middle school. Then, we practice—I give students a text, such as a short poem, and they try an RR. When finished, they share in small groups. Students are always surprised at the variety of their group mates' answers. We recap with a whole-group discussion of everyone's thoughts. Then they're off on their own, to begin a yearlong journey of exploration and reflection.

Reading Responses at Work

From Discussion to Essays,
and Uses for Reading Workshop

I cannot count the number of times in my teaching career that I've asked a whole class what students thought about a reading and one of the three following scenarios happens. Let's say we've just read Frost's "Stopping by Woods on a Snowy Evening." I ask the class, "Who has any thoughts about this piece?"

Scenario 1: No one raises a hand. A full minute goes by as I repeat the question in different and more specific words: "What did you think about this text? Did you notice anything? Any imagery, or anything about the form?" Eventually I call on someone.

Scenario 2: The student who always answers raises her hand immediately. When I call on her, she says that she liked it or didn't like it and gives a reason related to reading difficulty or length. Sometimes she might give a reason related to theme or plot, which I desperately seize upon and ask more questions about.

Scenario 3: I call on a student randomly, sooner rather than later. The student either says "I don't know" or has a brief answer such as "I didn't like it," which I try to probe.

Although my question is meant to empower students and let them direct the conversation, it is ineffective if students have not learned to read with presence and harness their thoughts. It presumes students have thoughts that are not only completely formed but also ready to be articulated. Students *do* have many thoughts, but those thoughts aren't necessarily cohesive or expressible immediately after reading something. Their blank stares don't automatically mean "I don't know"; they can mean something like "I could say something but I don't know where you want me to start and I don't want to look dumb." Once students learn how to access their own thinking in an articulate way, their sense of self-efficacy will increase and they will be able to have a discussion completely on their own, triggered by a question such as "What are your thoughts?"

If I had asked, "How many stanzas does this poem have?" or "What is the speaker in this poem doing?" I might have gotten a few more hands up. But the discussion would not be student directed; it would be focused on giving me the right answers I was looking for. In addition, the students who respond would most likely be the same three or four students who usually answer while the rest of the class waits—not just for the answer, but for the next activity, the next class, the next day. It is the opposite of learning with engagement and presence.

After one of the above conversations, the old me would show students a slide of some of the topics they should think about and then let them break into partners or groups to answer more questions.

Is this method terrible? No. Some students may have enjoyed the poem, or poetry in general, and would enjoy working on questions about it. Some would be motivated by grades or the satisfaction of pleasing the teacher to work hard on figuring the poem out, like a math problem to be solved. Some may not have cared about the poem at first but would become somewhat interested as they discussed the assigned questions with a group. Knowledge would be gained by most students, in varying degrees. It's not terrible. But rarely is a student genuinely engaged or excited to share a connection or well-formed opinion; rarely does a student have a question of his own to ask *me*.

Now it is different: When I know every student is sitting in his or her seat with at least one reading response prepared, and that there is a variety of specific, individually formulated ideas just waiting to be expressed—opinions, connections, questions, literary speculations, and all manner of observations, to name a few—I can facilitate the class in a myriad of ways, depending on factors such as textual difficulty, the class's personality and particular mood on any given day, and even simple daily variety. This chapter will describe the different facilitation moves I use.

Whole-Class Discussions

To get a larger discussion going, I first instruct students to have the text and their reading responses in front of them. I give them a minute to skim over their RRs to remember what they wrote, especially if the RRs were written a day or more before.

I've learned through experience that this thought-gathering time really helps students; they are better prepared to speak and listen to others when they've organized their own thinking. From there, I can lead a completely open-ended discussion or a more directed one, or, usually, a mixture of the two. Each is described next.

Open-Ended

This method can be done any time, but particularly works well for

- an easier or very brief text
- an eager and vocal class, or a class that has become vocal as the year goes on
- the beginning of a longer text, when students are just starting to get acclimated.

To start the discussion, I address the entire class with a question such as: "Let's hear what your thoughts are about this reading. Tell us what you wrote about in your RR. Take us anywhere in the text. Who wants to share first?" Of course, similar to the second scenario presented earlier, often the students who love to participate raise their hands. If that is the case, I can call on one of them to get the ball rolling, or I can choose a student randomly to explain his or her RR. The difference now is that I know the random student has a thought ready.

I can then guide the discussion in a few different ways (this is often called responsive teaching; I also call it teaching with presence). Let's say a student, Mollie, opens the discussion with the following: "I wrote an opinion about how I liked the rhyming in the poem and it made the poem nicer to hear and easier to understand." I would ask her to elaborate, to tell us which lines she cited, and to speculate on why Frost wanted to rhyme in the poem. From there, I could call on another student who had a hand up in the beginning, or who raises a hand after Mollie speaks. If no one is forthcoming, I might ask one of the following questions based on Mollie's contribution (see Figure 3–1).

Usually, as students start to participate, other students will spontaneously raise their hands to contribute. And as the discussion continues, I will offer comments and questions. With every new RR presented, I remind the class to flip to the lines cited by the student speaking. In this way, students move around the text, adding new thoughts to their existing annotations. As students become more comfortable with

Figure 3–1 *Decision Making When Teaching with Presence*

I might follow with	For this reason
Do people agree with Mollie? Does anyone disagree or want to change part of what she said?	I would ask this if the topic is debatable and I know more opinions are out there, or if I know Mollie said something about the text that was incorrect. A phrase like "change part of what she said" opens the door for a classmate to disagree without directly contradicting Mollie's entire answer, which a peer might be shy to do.
Who else wrote an Opinion RR like Mollie? What is your opinion?	I would ask this if I suspect other opinions exist, especially opposing ones. Mollie may have been accurate in her processing of the text—we don't need to revise or clear up Mollie's answer—but maybe the text lends itself to debate or at least multiple viewpoints.
Survey of hands: Who else liked the poem? Why did you like it?	This is a safe alternative for a class that seems afraid to answer and be wrong. I also might use a survey of hands if I sense that lots of students have the same strong opinion as Mollie, because I know they'll be eager to show it.
Mollie talked about the rhyme. Did anyone else notice the rhyme? What did you say?	This question takes Mollie's thoughts and transitions them into a new direction, which creates a sense of continuity in the discussion. It would be a good follow-up to the survey of hands, or for when I feel that all opinions have been explored. It is also a good way to start to crack open a difficult text. I try to focus the students not on the whole deeper meaning but on a more noticeable, structural aspect as a way in.
Mollie touched upon the form of the poem. Did anyone else notice something about the form?	I'm employing a similar logic as the question above, but this question is more difficult. I would ask this if I know the class already has a knowledge of some different elements of form.

this practice, they start to take over the conversation and I can fade in to the discussion as just another participant in the room.

By Category

Sometimes in a whole-class discussion, I start with a category in mind. I might do this at any time, but the method works particularly well for

- a more reticent class—students may feel more motivated to share if their category is solicited rather than with an open-ended invitation

- a complex or difficult text—starting with a certain category may break down elements of the text more easily

- a text with an obvious feature that would lend itself to a certain category.

When I start with a category in mind, I might ask, "Who wrote an Opinion RR about this text? Raise your hands." When the hands are up, I can call on someone while noting two or three other students to call on next. Another easy category to start with is Connection. I might ask, "Did this text remind you of anything else? Who has a Connection RR we can start with?" A third category that makes for an interesting discussion starter is the Joy of Genre. I try to refrain from telling students outright the genres of what we read—I want them to figure out the genre themselves using clues from the content and structure. (This was an incredibly hard habit to break! I am used to saying, "This is an article about . . ." or "Take a look at this poem by . . ." Now, I say, "Here's our next text . . ." or "Look at this reading; at first glance, what could it be?") If a student has written a Genre RR, we can begin by identifying the genre and discussing what makes it so.

As the discussion continues, I can zero in on any category and fully explore it. Often, this will depend on the difficulty level or any distinguishing features of the text. If a text is difficult, I might start by soliciting some of the easier categories such as Spot the Setting or Detect a Conflict. Later, as the discussion edges around the possible deeper meanings of the piece, I can ask the class who wrote Motivation, Theme, or Cultural Value RRs. And, with each new comment, I remind the class to add to their annotations.

Sometimes, even if text difficulty is not an issue, asking for specific categories facilitates discussion with a more reticent class or one that's just learning to discuss off what they've written in RRs. Let's say the class has read "The River-Merchant's Wife" by Li Po. I might ask, "Did anyone write about any of the literary criticisms here? This text has some wonderful possibilities for interpretation." Usually, at least one student has written a Feminist Criticism about the speaker of the poem. After soliciting any other Feminist Critiques, I would ask for others: "Did anyone write a Marxist or Psychoanalytical Criticism?" In keeping all the Criticism RRs together in one block of the discussion, students may not feel like they are branching off into new or risky territory; we are simply layering related ideas as we discuss. This scaffold often encourages a quieter class.

Of course, there is no guarantee that the RRs I inquire about are out there. But typically, they are, and if a student realizes that he may have been the only one to notice a theme, say, or the repetition in the last two lines, he feels motivated to share. In addition, as mentioned previously, once one student shares, her thoughts often suddenly jog other students' brains. It's not unusual for another student to raise her hand and say, "I didn't write about that but I was thinking the same thing as I read . . ." or "David's response reminds me of another book I read for book club . . ." Because choosing RR categories is completely up to the writer, students often feel a sense of coincidence or connection during the discussion. If they had only answered comprehension questions, everyone would know what everyone else wrote about. But with RRs, there are always surprises and correlations that arise organically. This gives whole-class discussions a flavor of discovery.

Classroom Culture

For any worthwhile discussion to happen, students must feel intellectually safe in the classroom. This means they know they won't be judged negatively for their contribution or bluntly corrected. During a whole-class RR discussion, students can become nervous about sharing their thoughts, even though they know it's not a right answer/wrong answer situation. From the beginning of the year, creating a culture of trust, openness, and encouragement—and one that appreciates mistakes—will help reluctant students be more willing to speak in front of everyone.

Small-Group or Partner Discussions

The structure I use most frequently for discussions is the small group. In a small group, each student becomes responsible for a large part of the discussion—she goes from being one-twenty-fifth of the input to one-fifth or more of it. And when the discussions start rolling, the energy level in the room increases palpably. Students let down their guard a bit and engage differently than they do in the larger group. This level of engagement leads to even more new ideas: As described with the whole-group discussion previously, the act of sharing RRs generates new connections and discoveries; this becomes multiplied in the small-group setting because of the number of small groups.

I put students with partners, or in smaller groups of three to five, and instruct them to take turns sharing their RRs with the group. Sometimes I let students choose their groups, and sometimes I randomly group them. Students find it easier to share in a small-group setting, especially if they are with friends, though random groupings can afford fresh perspectives. As with whole-class discussions, as each student speaks in the group, the others should turn to the cited portion in the text. I circulate around the class listening in and jotting notes.

To parlay these small-group discussions into a larger one, I wait until everyone has had a chance to share, and then instruct each group to select one RR from among them to be put forth to the whole class. This directive creates interesting discussions in the groups about which ideas would be the most interesting or informative to the whole class. Sometimes groups will ask to read two RRs if they are torn. Toward the end of class, I call upon each group, and the student designated to share gives his or her thoughts. This exercise can serve as an effective bit of summary or closure, and depending on how much time is left in class, I can use this whole-class portion to expand upon the groups' thoughts. As each group speaks, I can ask probing questions, solicit other connections, or survey the class, as described in the whole-group scenarios. The possibility for organic discussion and discovery is always present.

Another technique to gather the main points of different small-group discussions is to have one student in each group take minutes of the meeting by writing short notes about each student's RR. This student, or another, can then present the summaries at the end of class as a recap of the group's thoughts. And again, if time permits, I can expand these summaries through discussion to deepen the lines of thinking.

Summarizing an RR Versus Reading It

When students share their RRs, they can choose between summarizing the RR in their own words and reading the RR verbatim. Some students prefer a more informal discussion tone, and some like the security of reading what they have already written. In either case, the citation from the text should be clearly noted and read precisely. Often, students will silently read what they wrote first and then explain it in a more informal manner. This cycle of writing, rereading, and paraphrasing strengthens their thinking and speaking skills.

Mini–Reading Conferences

Many days, I have students share their RRs directly with me. While the class works on another task related to the reading, I circulate and have a short, focused reading conference over each student's RRs. This method gives me a chance to check that RRs are complete, as well as a chance to connect directly with each student. I also gather valuable information that I may not otherwise learn in a larger setting, about both individual and whole-class needs. For example, if many students have a similar question embedded in their RRs, or revealed in our one-on-one conversations, I'll know the topic needs more attention. Because students are sometimes reluctant to ask questions in front of their peers, the topic may not have been revealed otherwise. If an individual student is struggling with a literary concept or language convention, I can also informally monitor that journey through our one-on-one meetings as the issue arises.

Of course, talking to each student at his or her own desk reaps more than just knowledge about student understanding; there is a human element as well. Mingling through their desks, sitting or crouching beside each child, puts me among them and off "the stage." It sends the message that we are all in this together. I call the student by name, nod as she explains her thoughts, and engage in dialogue. I always find something genuine to praise, whether it be the original thought, quote, format, sentence structure, vocabulary, effort, or something else. I might delight in the student's connection; I might be able to answer the student's question. Often, the student proves to be the expert if he has written about another book or movie or hobby I don't know. It's a chance for me to learn something new about each student. Sometimes I'll jot down the student's thought and refer to it in the whole-class discussion, always giving the student credit. These small moments of connection add up and help build a classroom atmosphere of openness and trust necessary for genuine discussion and learning.

With my clipboard in hand, I begin on one end of the classroom and ask the first student, "What did you write about for your RR?" In this one-on-one situation, the student will usually summarize, but she may need a few seconds to reread the RR silently first. As she speaks, I look at her notebook to check for the criteria: length, category, quote, page, original thought. When she is finished, I can ask her a question, make a comment, or suggest an action such as rereading; the content of this teaching varies depending on the student's needs. Following are the most frequent topics I address during miniconferences.

Conferences Focused on Comprehension and Analysis

During these miniconferences, I learn much about student comprehension and depth of analysis. For example, if a student wrote a Tell the Theme RR about Gilgamesh's failed quest for immortality and subsequent personal growth, I'll know he understood that part of the story. If, on the other hand, a student wrote a Question RR about why Gilgamesh would try to drown himself in a river (he didn't, though he did purposefully sink himself to the bottom of a river to retrieve a plant), I'll know the student didn't understand that portion of the story. We can flip to that paragraph and reread together.

Similarly, if a student wrote a Question RR, I can try to direct her to an answer. Sometimes students' Question RRs are about something specific in the text, and sometimes they are broader or even philosophical. For example, while reading Chapter 1 of *The Outsiders*, a student might ask who Paul Newman was, and I can tell her to do a web search and then reread the passage. Another student might ask why teenagers feel the need to stereotype each other all the time. In this case, we could talk about existing evidence in the story as well as in real life. I could also ask her if she knew any other stories or movies with teens stereotyping each other. Her question would go unanswered but explored.

Conferences That Coach Students to Use Academic Language

When visiting each student individually, I also can help apply literary terms as needed. This is especially effective in a one-on-one situation, because students are less afraid to make mistakes and also cannot hide from what they do not know. Additionally, the individual conference allows the student to actually practice terms out loud in a safe setting.

For example, if a student wrote a Form and Content RR about the significance of a poem written in two-line stanzas, I would ask the student if he knows the specific name for those stanzas—*couplets*. Or, if a student wrote a Figurative Language RR about how exaggeration is used in a passage to create humor, we could discuss the term *hyperbole*. Similarly, if a student misused a term in her RR, I could redirect her. This happens often! One student, Josh, wrote an RR about a recurring theme in Confucius' "poems." When he was finished explaining it to me, I said, "You're exactly right about the theme—great job on that. But do you think these are poems?" We discussed why he thought they were (Confucius' sayings are short, and "sort of look like stanzas" when they are listed). But then we discussed what makes a poem. In the end, Josh realized they were separate sayings. I then upgraded that term to *aphorisms*.

Just as often as helping students with the meaning of literary terms, I help them with pronunciation. "This poem has a—a—caesar?" Meghan said while explaining her Figurative Language RR about a haiku by Basho. "Say-sure-a," I pronounced, pointing to the word *caesura* in her text. I had her say it again. I'm always amazed at how often this situation comes up—*I pronounced everything perfectly during my direct instruction*, I think to myself! But this is the point: Students need to practice academic language themselves, out loud. Merely hearing those terms or reading them silently may not be enough.

Conferences About a Student's Metacognitive Process

As noted in Chapter 2, a student's choice of category can reveal much about his thinking, and I often discuss category choices with students in miniconferences. As a student explains his RR, I will quickly mentally evaluate whether the category label fits the RR's content, and if it doesn't, or if it is an interesting or surprising choice, I will question the student about it.

It's rare that a student labels a response with a category that has nothing to do with the actual response, and if it happens, I simply question the student to discover the disconnect. More frequently, I question category choices out of curiosity. I am always interested in why a student chose one category over another category, for example. Similarly, I love to hear how and why students invent categories to fit their thoughts when they feel like the existing categories don't exactly apply. Or, I want to push the student who uses a category such as Give an Opinion or Significant Passage as a catchall to think more specifically about the kind of response she's written. In that case, I will question her about the content of her RRs until she arrives at a more precise label.

One student, Maddie, labeled an RR with the title Human Nature, which she created. Her response was about how Agamemnon "becomes human" in Book 9 of the *Iliad* when he must beg Achilles to rejoin the war. "Do you think that's just a character trait?" I asked her. "No, it's more . . . he changes," she said. "He becomes more of a real person in this chapter." In another class, Eryn used the existing Tell the Tone category to explore not Homer's tone in Book 9, but Agamemnon's: "I'm not talking about the tone of the writing," she explained, "but Agamemnon's tone—it changed dramatically here when he was trying to convince Achilles to come back. He wasn't arrogant and angry." Like Maddie, she felt it was more than just a character trait, and she had quoted appropriate dialogue to prove her point. I was intrigued and delighted; these students showed ownership for their learning and were not afraid to try something new. Discussions like these happen all the time when I conduct the one-on-one conferences.

Logistics

To visit each student, I assign the class any variety of other tasks to work on. They might read silently, work on analysis questions or an activity in groups, or complete another writing assignment. While they work, I make my way around to each desk. Though I keep the visits brief so I can get to everyone, sometimes the conferencing spills into two class periods. And even though we may only discuss one RR at each meeting, I will quickly check to see that any other RRs assigned that week (and discussed in other settings) are complete. If several RRs have been written since our last conference, I'll say to the student, "Choose one and tell me what you wrote." This allows the student to select what she is most proud of or interested in.

Online Discussions

Sometimes, I'll have students post their RRs to a forum such as Edmodo and require them to reply to at least two of their classmates. Although the "live" energy of a classroom discussion is missing, students are very comfortable with this format and usually enjoy the occasional change. I've also found that some students are more open to discuss their thoughts in an online forum than they are in person. Consider the following exchange about King Arthur's round table:

Leona P. to Eng II L2 Period 6

I have a question, don't laugh at me if I sound stupid! On page 53 paragraph #3, it says that "but before the knights of his court would be seated at the long table in the hall, a great strife broke out between them as to where they should sit." Why does it matter where they sit? Why would they get upset over something that little? Did they want to become closer to something? I'm so confused.

Leona would have never asked this in a whole-group, or even a small-group, setting. I should also note that this is a question I would not have asked in class, assuming that the idea of "the head of the table" was one everyone knew. I was glad Leona felt comfortable asking this question online. Her classmates helped her with their responses.

Nicole replied:

Leona, that isn't a stupid question because I was wondering the same thing as I was reading! It says after the part you said, "for they counted it a great honour to be near the head of the table than near the foot." I believe they were upset because the knights felt if they sat near the head of the table they were more honored than if they sat at the foot. They fought because they all wanted to be classified as a more honored knight.

Jovan replied:

Hey Leona that's not a stupid question at all. I see where you and Nicole are
coming from and I agree with you both. I mean, like I said in my quote why
must everything be a fight. Personally my opinion is, like you said why must you
fight about where you sit. At least you're able to sit at the "round table." This is
complete childish and immature behavior.

Nicole accurately touched upon the idea of a knight's seat reflecting his level of
honor, and Jovan questioned the cultural value of honor and rank. After reading
this, I asked the class who else was wondering about the significance of a round table
versus a rectangular table. To my surprise, over half the class raised their hands. We
took a few minutes to discuss the meaning of the custom and the possibly changing
cultural value.

As with other forms of discussion, after reading students' posts and replies, I can
highlight ideas to revisit with the whole class, make note of difficult passages, or list
terms to reexamine more closely. An online discussion setting works well not only as
a change of pace, but as a way to save in-class time if assigned for homework.

Polished Reading Responses

Every few weeks, I require students to turn in a polished RR. They must look
through the RRs they've written and select one to lengthen, type up, correct the
grammar, and turn in. This compels students to read through all of their recent
thoughts and choose one to revisit and deepen a bit more. In my class, polished RRs
should be a minimum of eight sentences—which, as with the regular RRs, can be
adjusted up or down depending on the class—and should have a clear beginning
and end. The RR should be a precise, encapsulated thought. The requirements are
as noted in Figure 3–2.

Having students periodically turn in a polished RR serves several purposes.
First, it gives students a chance to choose a piece of writing they'd like to think more
about, and to revise and edit what they've written. Perhaps something was discussed
in a small-group conversation or miniconference with me that the student can incorporate. Perhaps there is grammar or formatting that needs to be changed. At the very
least, the student must revisit and think further into the original idea to add three
sentences. Adding a title requires students to pinpoint both the topic and message of
the piece. Consider Emily's example on the next page.

Polished RR Protocol

- **Add at least three sentences.** Now that you have some distance from the RR, think about it some more and ask yourself how you can go even deeper into the thought. Can you explain another aspect or detail about it? Can you add another example?

- **Reword any parts of the RR that need it.** If any part is unclear, sloppily written, or too informal, reword it. If you used the first person, you can keep that, but change any slang or weak words such as *good*, *bad*, *great*, *excellent*, *thing*, and *kind of*.

- **Check the grammar.** Make sure all grammar and spelling is correct in the RR.

- **Keep all the RR parts.** Make sure your RR still has the category, quote, and page number within it. Format your quote and citation in MLA style. You do not need a works cited section.

- **Give it a title.** The title cannot be the RR category; it must point to your original thought. Having a title demonstrates control over the piece as a whole.

Figure 3–2 *Polished Reading Response Protocol*

Original RR

Mark the Motivation for the *Iliad*, by Emily, Grade 10

In Book 24, Priam is trying to get Hector's body back so he can have a proper transfer to the afterlife. After seeing how poorly Achilles has been treating Hector's body, Priam and his family have been very upset about it. On page 400 in lines 136–137 Priam says, "Revere the gods, Achilles! Pity me in my own right, and remember your own father! I deserve more pity." Throughout this passage, Priam's goal is to make Achilles feel sorrow for him by connecting it to his own life. Eventually, the decision is made to give Hector's body back to his family. In my opinion, this was an intelligent way to get his body back.

Polished RR

Uses of Pathos

As seen in the text, it is imperative that Priam receives his son's body from Achilles. This is crucial because of the firm belief in the transformation to the afterlife. On page 400 in lines 136–137 Priam says, "Revere the gods, Achilles! Pity me in my own right, and remember your own father! I deserve more pity." In these lines Priam is using pathos as a technique to make Achilles feel sorrow for him. Pathos is the quality or power in an actual life experience or in literature, music, speech, or other forms of expression, of evoking a feeling of pity, or of sympathetic and kindly sorrow or compassion. Priam is also trying to make the connection between him being a father and Achilles' own father. By doing this, he hopes Achilles will think about the situation from the opposite perspective. Eventually, Achilles gives Hector's body back, which means the technique Priam used was successful.

Notice that in the revised RR, Emily casts her original idea in a more refined light, using a term and its definition—*pathos*—we discussed in class. Substituting *imperative* for *trying to* better communicates the severity of the situation, and Emily entirely eliminates a weak sentence about the family being upset about the treatment of Hector's body. She makes her original idea about Priam trying to make a connection more specific, and by using *technique* instead of *intelligent way*, Emily makes Priam's tactics sound more deliberate. She also tightened up the final sentences from her original RR.

Collecting polished RRs like this every few weeks lets me give students more detailed grades and feedback without feeling overwhelmed. It allows me to help students more closely with grammar, spelling, sentence structure, word choice, and so on—things I would mention but not delve into during a mini–reading conference. At the same time, reading occasional sets of polished RRs is manageable work. By checking the flow of regular RRs with a detailed completion check (explained in Chapter 2), and giving written comments on polished RRs less frequently, I can keep students writing copiously and habitually, and provide consistent verbal and written feedback, without drowning in papers.

Reading Responses as Springboards for Essays

When it comes time for students to choose topics to explore in longer essays, I direct them to the RRs they have written over time. I might say something like this:

> *Every time you've written an RR, you've chosen the category. You've chosen the angle you wanted to work with. This means that something about that category, that angle, interested you. It was something you wanted to explore a bit more. Think about that. Could there be an idea in your RRs that you want to keep going with? Is there something that deserves more thought? Flip through your RRs and see if anything jumps out at you or sparks your interest again.*

I don't *require* students to write longer papers from RRs—they can choose their topics and formulate theses from new angles if they want—but paging through RRs gives them a place to start. This is important not only practically but psychologically:

Students aren't facing a completely blank page when tasked with beginning a longer, more formal essay. They have a collection of thoughts from which to begin, each with a head start of textual evidence built in.

The original thought in each RR is akin to a thesis—it is a thought that has been "proven" to some extent in the RR. A thesis, I tell students, is the same: an idea that must be explained and proven with reasoning and textual evidence in the course of the paper. If a student finds an RR that she'd like to explore further for a longer paper, she may be able to use the original thought in it as the actual thesis. Of course, it may need to be deepened, broadened, or sharpened a bit to sustain itself over a longer examination.

Consider the following example. Carlee asks a question about the legitimacy of Paris and Helen's marriage in an RR:

Ask a Question for the *Iliad* by Carlee, Grade 10

In the *Iliad*, I have questioned many times whether the marriage between Paris and Helen was legitimate. She never formally divorced Menelaus, so she is in some sort of a marriage triangle. Did she divorce Menelaus? And is she legally married to Paris? I read on Wikipedia, "In ancient Athens, both husband and wife had the power to initiate a divorce. The husband simply had to send his wife back to her father to end the marriage. For the wife to obtain a divorce, she had to appear before the archon." So, we know that Menelaus did not initiate the divorce, because Helen was forcibly taken from him. We also know that Helen could not have initiated divorce, because the archon, or monarch, was Menelaus, and as before mentioned, he did not want the marriage to end.

Carlee became so interested in this question that she decided to write her essay about it. In the essay, she further researched marriage customs in ancient Greece. Here is the beginning of her essay:

Who Is Helen's Husband?

The *Iliad* can be viewed as a story of war, a story of anger, a story of the gods, or a story of love. The events seem to be based off of the "love triangle" of Helen, Paris, and Menelaus. Helen's marriages appear to be partial—in the legal aspect, she is married to Menelaus. In a loving and feeling aspect, she is married to Paris. The question that would appear to frequent the minds of readers is this: Who was Helen really married to?

Carlee's paper went on to examine legalities of marriage in ancient Greece, the role of love, and even textual clues such as Helen's referring to Priam, Paris's father, as "father-in-law." She incorporated outside research and quotes from the text throughout. At the end of the paper, she outlined Greek divorce proceedings, stemming from the original quote she found for her RR. She then concluded:

> Ultimately, it can be assumed that in a way, Helen was still married to Menelaus, but in her opinion she was married to Paris. So, it really depends on the side that the reader chooses. If the reader believes a marriage is a legal matter, then Helen is married to Menelaus. If the reader believes that a marriage is about love and feeling, then Helen is married to Paris. It is left to interpretation.

Had Carlee not been given the small space of an RR to formulate the question, she may not have experienced the process of thinking deeply about and researching a topic she really enjoyed. She became so invested, in fact, that at the end of the *Iliad* unit, when students were required to create an imaginative project for the text, Carlee made a wedding scrapbook for Helen and Menelaus!

As Carlee's writing demonstrates, students may have to make a shift from a less formal, personal style into a more formal, academic style when converting an RR into a longer essay. This is a teachable moment about purpose, audience, and genre.

Whether students use an RR as a seed for a longer essay or not, the experience of paging through all they've written so far, seeing the volume of their own thoughts and writing, is a confidence booster. Students usually dread the thought of a longer paper, but I tell them, "You've been doing this the whole time. Find a thought you'd like to run with, and then go to the text. You know how to do this."

Reading Responses and Reading Workshop

Any of the methods explained previously are appropriate to use in both a traditional literature class and a reading workshop setting. When students are reading the same text, RRs explore several facets of that text at once, enabling students to view the text from different angles. In a reading workshop setting, the students haven't necessarily read each other's texts, but this gives rise to new explorations and builds required skills.

For example, let's say the class has written RRs about self-selected books and are in small groups to share. A student might explain the importance of a setting in a certain chapter, but to anchor the thought in context, she would also have to summarize part of the plot or explain the symbolism of a certain space. The student, in effect, becomes the teacher of the work for the group, giving background knowledge and information about characters, motives, plot, and so on. She is the expert.

Of course, when hearing about a new book, other students might become interested in that book for themselves. After an RR is presented, the discussion often twists and turns in several directions as the group inquires more about the book. Sometimes these are questions about

- **Genre:** So this book is a murder mystery?
- **Plot:** What happens after the crash?
- **Point of view:** Wait, so the boy is the actual narrator?
- **Writing style:** Is it easy to read or does it get boring?

or any other topic—questions arise naturally and the discussion transforms from a teacher-mandated sharing session to a high-energy, high-interest, organic book chat. The conversation becomes one of natural exploration and curiosity. This, in turn, demands more of the speaker—he must be able to address all manner of queries about the book.

Does the previous scenario happen in every reading workshop RR discussion? No—but it happens frequently, and when it does, it's magical. Students walk away with ideas for their next book choices, or at least with an exposure to the many books available to them and the many stories that exist in our world. This exposure in itself is important: Students realize that they belong not only to a world of events, but also to a community of readers and thinkers, each of them reading and reporting on books of their own choosing. And acquiring information about other books via RRs serves as a solid foundation from which to consider these books—students get concrete, meaningful ideas instead of hearing vague musings about liking a book or thinking it was good.

One of my students, Madison, told me that workshop books were easier to discuss with RRs as a scaffold for the conversation: "It was easier to say what we were thinking . . . the discussion was more specific." Richard said writing RRs for his workshop book was harder than writing a book review (a routine assignment with the workshop books). "I had to think more about it," he said. "I couldn't just say general things. I had to find a spot to use as a quote." He agreed, though, that it made the discussion better. With RRs, students have better access to their own thoughts. This not only elevates conversation, but creates it. Years ago, when I first started incorporating reading workshop in my class, the discussions felt superficial and obligatory; with RRs as the catalysts, they have become lively and natural, and they end with students excited to investigate new books they learned about from their peers.

Endless Possibilities

When students have specific, cited, categorized thoughts written out and ready to be shared, class time becomes a time of meaningful discovery. Students do not passively ingest information but actively create it through their own interaction. The role of the teacher becomes one of backstage facilitation, expert clarification, and joyful encouragement. RRs are like cinder blocks—small and concrete, manageable for one person to carry. But when used together, all manner of building becomes possible.

Above and Beyond

Metacognitive Investigation with the Reading Response Analysis Paper

After working with RRs for a while, I began to notice that in general, students liked some categories more than others, and specific students each had their own preferences as well. The students noticed it, too: I would stop by Cary's desk for a mini–reading conference and he would say, almost apologetically, "I wrote another Connection—I don't know what it is about connections. I just love making them. I see them so easily."

"That's a good thing," I told him. "Not everyone can do that. It means you can link themes or traits across stories in your mind and see larger patterns. It's a handy skill to have." Another student, Emily, remarked, "I know I ask a lot of questions. But I can't help it—they just pop into my mind." And Cara once told me, "None of my friends like writing Figurative Language responses. I know it's weird, but I really enjoy talking about similes and metaphors and imagery."

Of course, it's not weird at all—students think differently based on their aptitudes, interests, prior knowledge, and a million other factors. But these occasional remarks got me thinking: What if all students could notice real patterns in their mental preferences and processes using RRs? By the end of a semester, students had dozens of RRs in their notebooks—on one hand, it was four months' worth of literary criticism and intellectual growth; on the other, it was data. What if they looked through it and drew some conclusions?

Thus, the reading response analysis paper was born.

I assign the RR analysis paper at the end of each semester, and it serves as both a powerful self-assessment and an effective review for our midterm or final test. It started out with only a few reflective questions on it, but grew as I began to consider the nuances involved in reading, choosing something to write about, and writing.

The paper has two main parts. First, students work their way through several questions directing them to reflect on their RR habits and preferences. In the second part, students must select their five "best" RRs thus far in the year and retype them. Below each selected RR, students must write one or two sentences about *why* they think the RR was effective.

When I assign this paper, I assure students that there are no "right" answers; there is only reflection and effort. I explain to them that knowing *how* one thinks can help in all subjects and even throughout life. Being able to step back from one's own brain is a skill that must be practiced to be strengthened and can yield important insights about habits and learning.

Section 1: Reflection

This section of self-analysis asks students to reflect deeply about their RR writing to this point in the year. Typically, students will have almost two typed pages or more when finished. I tell them that there is no limit on length, but each category of questions works well as its own paragraph. Normally, I would not make a reflection paper so structured, but I have found that the more specific questions I provide, the richer the answers and deeper the contemplation. I ask students to look back at the RR guidelines they received in the beginning of the year and consider the following questions as they analyze themselves as readers and responders. The reflection must have at least five paragraphs.

Part 1: Process

- How do I write RRs? Do I read all the way through first, and then find something to write? Do I write as soon as an RR pops into my head? Do I begin reading with a category in mind? Is it a mix of these? Explain.

- Am I mostly summarizing, or is there clear evidence of my own original thoughts in the RRs? Is this difficult for me? Did this change over the semester? How?

I want students to reflect on the first set of questions for the sake of curiosity; by becoming aware of the order in which they think, students can eventually try to use the order to their advantage, instead of simply "getting it done." Most students read a passage all the way through, jotting small notes for possible RRs, and use one of those ideas to write full RRs. Other students write out whole RRs the minute an idea pops into their head. But some students use RRs strategically. In her paper, Morgan explained that she reads the entire piece first and then goes back to think of a reading response that she can use to help her understand the meaning of the text better. She consciously tries to use RRs to dissect a difficult or cloudy aspect of the text, and therefore she reads the whole way through first.

My question about summarizing has a motive. From my experience, I know that many students in fact mostly summarize in the beginning of the year, and then grow in thinking ability, confidence, and voice as time goes on. This results in more original thought. However, I want students to realize this on their own. In his paper, Clay explained it this way: "In the beginning of the semester, I summarized and used the author's thoughts more than the thoughts of my own. I feel that this has changed over the semester in that I began incorporating more of my own thoughts. It has gotten easier to translate my thoughts from my head onto paper." Lauren described a similar change: "I found it easier at the beginning of the year to just state what was happening in the reading. Over the semester I found it was more beneficial to write what I was thinking so the response could go even deeper than the required elements." Many students will write some version of this idea. By noticing for themselves the power of their own thoughts, students will hopefully become more confident in their abilities and further committed to developing their voice.

Part 2: Type

- Which kinds of RRs do I gravitate to? Which kinds of RRs do I like most? Why? Which do I like least? Why?

- Do I always write the same kind of RR? Do I have a variety?

- Is there a certain kind of RR that I've never tried? Why might this be so?

With these questions, students must think about the categories of RRs that they seem to prefer, based upon what they've written so far. Most students will know the answer to this without consulting their work; it's the "why" portion of the questions that give them pause. The third section of questions goes deeper into the "why," but here, I want students to first *notice* that they may have pathways of thinking that they feel comfortable traveling in.

Many students will admit their fondness for Give an Opinion, Make a Connection, or Ask a Question RRs, because these are traditionally the most used categories. Emily spoke for many of her peers when she wrote:

> I enjoy giving my opinion because I find that easiest. I will always have an opinion on whatever reading I do, meaning if I like it or not. Next, I choose ask a question because I always wonder about what I am reading. There is almost always a portion that I don't understand, so this helps me get my thoughts out. Also, make a connection is a simple one. This way I can connect the reading to my own life, which helps me better understand the situation at times.

Many students, however, like these categories for different reasons. Andrew likes connections not because they are easy but because if he can "trigger an emotion or a memory" about the reading, it "tends to stay in my head longer." Blanca almost always asks questions because she realized that when she reads, "a lot of questions come to my head." She likes to see if she can answer it herself by the end of the passage. Joe writes opinions for the discussion possibilities: "I enjoy being able to argue my beliefs against a wide variety of other arguments that can also very well be true."

Of course, a predilection for opinions, connections, and questions is not always the case. Some students prefer writing about language, mood, foreshadowing, or characters: These seem obvious to them. Some students get very excited about archetypes; some can't wait to try the literary criticisms. Sawyer is partial to themes: "I find looking for themes both fun and interesting," he explained. "It is like getting inside the author's head and recreating the motion of the cogs." And Eryn "forces" herself to use different categories each time: "I like to use more of a variety of reading response categories, as I get bored using the same ones over and over. I think it benefits my writing to choose different kinds."

Students will also easily be able to answer which categories they *don't* like. The reasons vary—perhaps they view a category as too difficult, too obvious, or too boring. I try to use this information to individually help or challenge them in class. I want students to realize that there is value in pushing oneself out of one's comfort zone. One high-achieving student, Destiny, revealed why she doesn't write Language Recognition RRs: "I find language recognition to be more difficult to write about. Not only this, but it is also typically unimportant in the understanding of the passage." When I read this, I made a note to help Destiny better recognize and understand figurative language in our texts.

Part 3: Metacognition

- What stands out for me when I read? What is difficult for me to see?

- What am I most interested in when I read?

- Do I take risks in thinking when I respond to readings? How?

- Do I play it safe with my thinking? How?

- Am I afraid to be wrong? Why or why not?

- Do I enjoy challenging myself as a reader? Do I think I am a strong reader?

- Do I feel confident in my abilities to respond in some way to a reading, even if I don't understand it 100 percent?

I am often surprised at the level of perception students will use when responding to these questions. For example, consider Joe's reflection:

When I write my RRs, I sometimes notice a couple attributes that make me a strong and also a weak reader. I will find myself going very in depth with a topic, more than I ever thought I could. Other times I will go way off topic and when we present in class, my response seems so wrong it was surprising I read the same story. I believe this happens simply because I try and complicate stories and their meanings. When it comes to a very simple story with a theme way out in the open, I can expect myself to come up with some elaborate explanation about how the theme is hidden and why a character does something when really it isn't as complicated as I am making it.

By noticing the way he thinks when he reads, Joe is honing his skills for future readings. He will be asking himself, *Am I overthinking this?* and hopefully will search the text for evidence and answers. He "can expect [him]self" to think a certain way, but now he will question it. Instead of simply reacting to readings unconsciously, Joe has intercepted his habitual thought patterns.

Students make a variety of observations. Dani remarked about her penchant for philosophical thinking: When she looks at herself "as a writer and thinker," she notes that "my category choices speak in volume. I enjoy expanding on the philosophical ideas and I find it easy to generate original thought when considering something that is abstract." Hannah realized she easily finds technical aspects of the readings: "The types of reading responses that I choose reveal that I pay attention to what type of language and literary devices [the authors] use." Mikayla likes "the crossover topic because I always understand the piece so much more when I notice how certain literary devices affect others" but then noted that she has "more difficulty with the ones that are about the structure of the piece. For example, I have a harder time spotting the climax and claim rather than the symbols and archetypes." And Josh questioned his very personality: "I could say that since I have so many opinions I must have an ego problem and think I'm always allowed to chime in on things, or I can look at it and think about how I can generate original thoughts about almost anything." These acknowledgments become strengths for the students; in verbalizing *how* they think, they can begin to focus on going beyond their comfort zones.

Some students, like Nina, don't mind mistakes in their RRs. "Recently in one of my responses, I completely misinterpreted the piece we were reading," she wrote, and then noted, "I am not afraid of interpreting [the passage] wrong." And Destiny felt that her actual willingness to make mistakes is what makes her a strong reader: "I try to think of the author's reasoning behind their thoughts and I am not always right," she wrote. "I am confident in my suggestions, although I might be wrong, and for this I am a strong reader."

But despite my efforts and constant reminding that there are no wrong answers with RRs, many students will reveal in their analyses that they are still afraid to be wrong with their responses and often play it safe. I can only guess that this is a result of ingrained thinking and simple human nature. I comfort myself with the thought that at least they *realize* they're playing it safe and admit to it—perhaps someday they will be willing to try greater risks. One measure I've implemented to encourage more risk-taking is to declare a round of RR writing as a "Take a Risk" round, for which everyone "must write something they would never normally write," or "something they think is probably 'out there,'" I tell them. This helps to nudge students a bit to the next level.

But playing it safe doesn't always mean what I expect. Sawyer, the student who prefers writing about themes, does not like writing connections or questions because of "a fear of being incorrect in my connection or interpretation. I know that questions technically contain no real wrong answers, but I would rather do another category rather than risk seeming as if I am uneducated on what I am talking about." For him, playing it safe means writing about themes! And Masen wrote that the entire RR process is a kind of safe zone, so it's impossible *not* to be safe: "I don't really 'take risks' in my writing because writing in this private atmosphere presents no risk; it is simply myself and my words." Katja agreed: "I am deathly afraid of being wrong. But I am OK with being wrong on paper."

Finally, students often note a rise in confidence as readers and writers, even while realizing they are not perfect. Masen explained that "even if the entire meaning, theme, and plot all go right over my head, I can still extract a single line to interpret, or a literary pattern I notice, or something grammatical. This is one of my most prevalent strengths as a writer." This is one of the goals of the RR practice—the recognition of deep reading as a process that may take time but is not impenetrable.

Part 4: Surprises and Changes

- Have I ever been surprised (or surprised myself) when writing an RR? How so?

- Has my RR writing changed over the course of the semester? How so?

- Have my reading habits changed as a result of writing RRs? How so?

With these questions, I want students to consider how the act of writing reveals thinking. I also want them to notice how they've changed over the course of the semester. Students universally remark that they are surprised by (1) writing more than they ever thought they could and (2) writing ideas or language that sounds more intelligent than students think they are. Emily voiced the thoughts of many:

> When I was first told I was going to have to write reading responses throughout the year, I thought it was going to be very difficult. As a week or two passed, I noticed how easy it was for me to pick up on things in the story and write about them. This had me in shock because I was never creative or good at writing.

Aidan was also surprised at the quality of his writing: "When I have written my responses, I have actually surprised myself . . . This is because I don't see myself as a very strong writer but sometimes I'm impressed by my writing. I think of words that I never thought I'd see myself using." Similarly, Hannah noted, "When I'm done writing, it is far better than I thought it was going to be. From a writing perspective, I see myself expanding my vocabulary and using a more mature writing style." And Madison said, "There were several instances where I started writing a reading response and then completely changed my idea and it ended up being a lot better than I had anticipated . . . I really like when this happens because it makes me feel like I am a better reader than I give myself credit for."

I see remarks like these again and again in the RR reflection papers, and they are gratifying to read. I constantly tell the students that the act of writing creates new thought, that practicing writing makes us better writers, that our brains are smarter than we think if we give them a chance—but students don't believe these maxims until they see for themselves. Having students write RRs consistently, and look back on what they've written, shows them. There is something about the RR structure that seems manageable and nonthreatening to students; the safety net of the RR parameters, and the narrow focus of RRs, takes the pressure off students to produce intellectually dazzling interpretations of texts and to simply write what they think. When that happens, they create a space for their brains to work.

Some students do think they are capable writers, but are still surprised by the volume of writing produced with RRs. Anthony said, "At first, I wasn't sure how I could write a paragraph every night, but then I created a system that helped me understand the story, while creating topics for my reading response." Olivia noted an improvement in ideas: "I might've had trouble coming up with something to write about—especially if I didn't entirely understand the reading—but that rarely happens anymore."

Some students notice that instead of writing more, they've learned to write less. Abby explained that she realized she "did not have to write one page to get my point across. I can make it one paragraph and use new vocab and fine sentence structure, while having the same effect as I did for the one-page response." Or, students have learned to write more genuinely. Katya noted, "My RR writings sound a lot less forced now because I write what I want to write about, not what I think I should write about."

Many students illustrate the precept that writing is an extension of thought. Linley, for example, was surprised at her ability to figure out answers while she wrote. "Many times as I've written my responses, I have surprised myself with what I came up with," she explained. "For example, there have been instances where I had asked a question that at first did not make sense to me, and as I worked through my response I had realized I'd ended up answering it." Kylie explained that sometimes she starts an RR and changes it "halfway through. I start writing, and realize things I did not realize until I put my thoughts on paper, and then I want to go in a different direction." In Joe's case, it wasn't so much a matter of extending thought as much as simply capturing thought: "Writing some of these responses I found opinions that I didn't even know I believed in before writing it. When I write, my mind moves a million miles per hour and I believe that my true thoughts come down on the paper, which is why this shocked me so much." Of course, we as teachers know these moments to be true. When writing consistently as a practice, and then reflecting on what they've done, students become convinced on their own.

Sometimes students note a confidence in ideas that carries over into the discussion. Blanca described it this way:

Sometimes I start thinking about a simple reading response and I end up writing about a very deep theme and when I finish I don't even remember how I got to that point of understanding. The next day in class we talk about the reading and we analyze it there are a lot of times when we talk about a specific part of the story and I get surprised because it was what I wrote my RR about and that makes me feel proud and realize that little by little I'm getting better.

This happens often—during a class discussion a student will suddenly pipe up with "That's what I wrote my response about!" Each of these small encounters, these moments of revelation, contribute to a student's sense of self-efficacy in reading and writing.

Most students will admit that not only do they become more fluent and thoughtful writers, but that they become more careful readers as well. Emily remarked that "since we have had to write [RRs], I have been annotating the stories more thoroughly. This helps me better understand the story overall, as well as understanding the small details." Andrew described his quality of thinking while reading: "I think more in depth than I did in the beginning of the year. Also, when a quote that comes across me interests me, I think of more than one way to interpret it, and try to view it from more sides than just my own." And Aiden surprised himself with his new level of engagement when reading. "Thinking and engaging myself with the text is also something I feel I've strengthened," he wrote. "I most definitely have surprised myself by seeing and connecting concepts I never thought would be connected, and I'm doing this while I'm reading." Lauren, on the other hand, has improved her reading not necessarily through the writing of RRs but through the discussion of them: "By listening to other reading responses, I am influenced to change how I think while reading. I have started to analyze my thought process and how I can improve it."

Morgan was surprised by the times she missed the mark: "One thing that surprises me is when I write a reading response at home and then come into school and what I thought was wrong. I will think that I know what the story or poem was about, but then it will be the opposite of what I wrote." This too is a powerful realization and a potent learning moment.

And then there are random surprises that have nothing to do with the act of reading or writing. Masen surprised herself with the amount of emotion that comes forth when writing connections: "Sometimes I can connect to a topic so deeply," she wrote, "I'm amazed that someone else [i.e., the author] could feel something so similar to me. I remember that experiences and emotions can be universal . . . Reading responses have woven together literature and reality for me." Andrew told this story: "One time I was discussing a memory I had from 2–3 years ago in my life, and while writing I actually realized I was going through the same thing now. I had no idea that reading 'The Fisherman and the Jinnee' could ever make me think that way, and I rethought some of my actions after it." The act of writing, if done with presence, opens something in both the mind and heart, regardless of the initial topic or purpose.

Sometimes, to my great joy, a student will note that he "thinks" in reading responses when reading—that the practice of writing RRs has trained his brain to constantly look for possible RR topics. Clay wrote that while reading, "I feel like I am writing RRs in my head whenever I see an important part of the literature." Ryan noted that "instead of just reading assigned readings to simply 'get through them,' I now read looking for symbols and elements to write my reading responses about." Sawyer realized that he notices more literary techniques as he reads, even when RRs are not required: "I've become more aware of things such as simile, themes, foreshadowing, etc. in different readings. Even outside of English, I'll accidently make mental notes of things to mention in my reading response." Of course, it is no accident! When writing RRs consistently, students develop a sort of "muscle memory" for dissecting texts; they can't help but do it all the time.

Although most students sharpen their analyzing skills, others learn to learn to relax a little. Katya, a straight-A student and self-described perfectionist, explained that through writing RRs, she has released her need to overanalyze and overannotate every line of a text, and instead has freedom to simply read, allow the text to reveal itself naturally, and let her mind formulate a thought about what she actually wants to write about. "This makes me put more emotion into my work, which actually helps me understand the passage better," she wrote. This "emotional connection" way of thinking has helped her outside of English class as well: "I have applied this philosophy to my other classes . . . and it has actually resulted in most of my highest grades yet."

Part 5: Looking Back, Looking Ahead

- Am I trying my best when I write RRs? How could I be putting more thought and effort into them?

- As I move in to the next semester, what new things could I be thinking about or looking for as I read?

Many students believe they are putting their best effort in, but still want to improve. Ashley explained, "I am putting my best effort into my RRs. I do this so it's easier for me to understand the text, and to study for tests." But then she noted that she "could be putting more personal thought into them. I seem to always think logically" instead of making deeper personal connections.

But some students, although they meet or exceed the requirements for writing RRs each day, will say that they aren't trying their hardest, or that they've reached a plateau. Sometimes students admit they are doing the minimum for the grade. As with every other part of the reflection paper, the act of verbalizing this is a potential catalyst for change. The pull toward completing the minimum requirement will always be a factor, not only with RRs but with any other assignment. I've tried to combat this by making the minimum requirements specific and challenging, and if I feel an entire class needs more of a challenge I can up the ante by requiring more RRs, longer RRs, or RRs with two quotes instead of one. However, the easiest way to reengage students who have mastered the minimum requirements is to give more RR category choices. I have found that by adding more challenging categories as the year progresses, and requiring students to regularly select from the new categories, students feel a renewed sense of effort and stimulation.

In terms of improving in the future, students usually talk about challenging themselves with different categories, or taking risks in some way: "I think that in the next semester I want to try and branch out and get a little bit out of my comfort zone because I'm eventually going to need to learn how to take risk without the fear of being wrong," Keena wrote. Similarly, Tamane noted that as she moved into the next semester, she "could be thinking of taking more risks and reflecting upon my fear of being wrong, trying out a diversity of types of responses." Or, students will talk about their level of original thought: Although they use some in each RR, they want to use more, to develop more of a unique voice. Whatever the goal, when students can visualize and verbalize what growth looks like, they set themselves on the path of reaching it.

Just as writing RRs makes students realize what they did not know about a text, writing the RR reflection paper makes them realize what they did not know about themselves. Students see that they are developing the habits of curious, critical, informed readers. Linley very eloquently explained it this way:

> These activities help me outside of English due to the process of thought I have
> developed . . . I can now read at a much quicker pace and still be able to
> understand the material. This has lead me to enjoy reading much more . . . I

cannot say that I have always been excited to write [RRs], but I have always been excited about seeing their results. I have also learned to be confident in my opinion and to write about what I believe. I now do not want to have the same idea as everyone else; I enjoy sharing ideas that are unique to my morals and interests. Lastly, these reading responses act as an outlet for creativity and intelligence. They help students in both school and life on a much larger scale than it may seem at first glance. Reading responses shape us to be determined, articulate, and insightful human beings.

When students voice their thought processes, they own them. They become more confident with reading in general and their ability to face any text. They detect areas that need growth and name them. And, hopefully, they start to believe that not fully understanding a text, especially on a first read, is not only acceptable but expected—and it certainly won't diminish the skills they know they already have.

Section 2: Five Best Reading Responses

For the second part of the paper, students must skim through all of the reading responses they've written over the course of the semester, identify their five strongest responses, type up (or copy and paste) those responses, and write two or three specific and thoughtful sentences about *why* they think each response is strong. My hope is that by focusing on existing strengths, students will notice growth, feel confident, and recommit themselves to the process. Here is an example of one of Dani's five best RRs about an ancient Chinese poem, and her commentary.

Sensing a Symbol for
"Thick Grow the Rush Leaves"

In this song the speaker is in search of someone. The speaker travels upstream, but only succeeds in finding what they are looking for when traveling downstream with the current. Line 5 says, "I went up the river to look for him but the way was difficult and long." The river symbolizes fate and the boy the speaker is looking for symbolizes something she wants. Going against fate is hard, as is traveling upstream against the current. The speaker finds what she is looking for when she trusts fate, and travels downstream.

Comments: This is definitely my favorite reading response I have written. This symbol recognition is strong because it acknowledges the bigger picture. Most symbols I find are a small object or a minor character. However, in this response the entire poem is a symbol including the plot, setting, and characters. It also symbolizes the philosophical effects of fate on a character trying to reach a boy in a river. Being able to expand on fate also made this a strong response.

Dani realized she had touched upon something deep and important in the poem and did not make just a surface-level observation. Often, students will select the "best" RRs based on the actual thinking demonstrated in the RR or the depth of literary analysis. Other comments like this include:

- "Before this year, I knew nothing about other cultures. This response shows how much I've learned and how I applied my new knowledge to other works."

- "This RR is strong because it isn't a connection between two stories that are the same. It talks about how the two stories differed and how they reflect each other."

- "I think this RR was good because I really demonstrated my understanding of that character."

- "I like how I connected such an old poem to modern-day morals."

- "This RR touched upon a theme we have been talking about all year."

- "After writing this response I feel as if making this connection thinned the cultural divide that I believed existed."

Many times, students will choose RRs they felt they put much effort into, and give that as the reason for the strength of the RR. Or, students will feel proud about stepping out of their comfort zones, as Maddie did:

> ### Ask a Question/Cultural Values for "The Fisherman and the Jinnee"
>
> Reading "The Fisherman and the Jinnee," I kept in mind the Western stories that emerged from these stories. In many of them, there is a genie (jinn). When we think of genies, we often relate them to bringing great joy. When you rub the bottle, the genie is released and they do a good deed. Often we think of them granting three wishes. I wondered why in "The Fisherman and the Jinnee," he did the opposite. Instead of granting a reward, the Jinnee said, "Choose the manner of your death and the way I shall kill you" (pg. 88). I wondered if this came before good jinnees, after them, or if Western stories were created with our values in mind to appeal to a greater audience.
>
> **Commentary:** For this reading response I really thought deep about how our cultures connected. Despite not knowing for sure if I was right, I took a personal "risk" and asked a question.

Sometimes students will remark on the RR process itself. Maybe they are proud of trying a new category or even inventing a category. "I really like how I created my own category," Carlee wrote. "It was a different way to include my own thoughts." Or they will feel proud about their use of an apt quote, sound reasoning, or a particular detail: "This is one of my best reading responses because I paid attention to detail. I didn't just pass over this sentence thinking nothing of its weird wording," Ryan explained. Frequently, students will feel proud about something that occurred during the actual writing of the RR:

- "This RR is a specifically strong writing because it covers a theme that I would not have uncovered had it not been for the writing of this response."
- "When I read the passage, I really didn't know what it was saying, but with [writing out] this interpretation, it helped clear it up. I truly believe in what I wrote and just let my hand do the writing to explain myself."
- "This RR is strong because I asked a question and proposed an answer by the end."

Sometimes, students will note the change in writing or thinking that has transpired over the course of the semester. "This response shows just how far I've come in my responses," Josh wrote. Kylie commented: "This RR shows how I've grown in my RRs. Now that I go more in depth and look for symbols, I believe that this has allowed my understanding of the story to expand as well as my writing."

I'm often surprised at the some of the reasons students give for thinking an RR is strong—not that I disagree, but that students frequently think or notice things that I do not. Joe, for example, wrote about why he appreciated an RR that was actually dead wrong:

> The reason I liked this one so much is because it is simply just misguided. I honestly got the theme wrong and I realized that after I was finished reading but decided to keep it because it reminded me how up for debate these pieces can be . . . In this case the text is mostly talking about how some people can only see certain sides to the story while I thought that it had to do with making false claims. I really liked this one simply because it was funny to me how wrong a person can be while still having a good point.

Overwhelmingly, however, students feel their best RRs were the ones they felt an emotional connection to when writing them. For example:

- "I think I write my best when passionate about something."
- "This was a very special response to me simply because of how much I identify with the theme."
- "What truly made my reading response strong was I was able to express my thoughts, and I have noticed that when I express my thoughts and have a strong opinion on something, I write so much better."

By pinpointing specific reading responses they felt were strong, students acknowledge and highlight what success looks like for them. They can feel proud about what they've done so far, and set the bar for themselves for the future.

Confucius said that the noblest path to wisdom is through reflection. And John Locke believed that education begins a person, but "reading, good company, and reflection must finish him" (Ireland 2017, 61). The practice of reading with RRs in mind, writing, discussing, and looking back on what one has done through the reflection paper aims to push students in the direction of genuine growth. They not only read with presence, they *realize* they read with presence, and thus, think with presence—a skill that will carry over into every area of their lives.

Part Two

Reading Response Categories and Examples

My family and I spent New Year's 2018 visiting Boston, a special trip that included something for everyone. My goal was to simply walk the Commons and soak in the city air; my husband, Tim, had bought tickets for a special *Looney Tunes* presentation by the Boston Pops; our sons had received Celtics tickets for Christmas. Before we set out for the game, I pulled back the drapes on our thirty-sixth floor hotel room and exclaimed, "Look at how beautiful it is!" I was referring to the Charles River in the sunset. Tim said, "I know! It's a supermoon!" and my sons said, "Cool! How did they get the '18' on the building?" (The Prudential Center had a giant "18" in a perfectly lit pattern in its windows.) We were all looking out through the exact same hotel-sized window, and yet we each immediately assumed beauty in different directions.

This is how each person goes through life—with his or her own perspective, feelings, interests, background, and hopes—even when we are looking at the same thing. So it is with students. They cannot help but see through a personal lens. But with the tools to clarify their thoughts, they can share their perspectives and teach one another. When I told Tim and the boys that I was referring to the Charles turned purple and peach, they noticed it too. I myself marveled at the moon and the "Pru."

I see this phenomenon in class all the time. Once, when a small group was discussing the Hebrew short story "The Book of Ruth," they realized with delight that they had each separately written a different RR about the *same lines* in the story. When Ruth's mother-in-law tells Ruth to go home to her own family, Ruth replies, "Wherever you go, I will go. Wherever you lodge, I will lodge. Your people shall be my people, and your God my God." Mikayla wrote a Language Recognition RR about parallelism; Ashley wrote a Seeing the Significance RR about the pivotal moment in the plot; Maddie wrote a Character Description RR about Ruth's loyalty; Keena wrote about Ruth's intentions in a

Mark the Motivation RR. Each student had thought her own response was the obvious one. Each marveled at the insightful perspective of her peers.

In Part 2, you will see a diversity of thought from a beautiful group of student minds through the use of the RR method. The examples in these chapters show students thinking deeply and authentically about a rich variety of texts, old and new, from both whole-class and independent reading. They make meaningful connections and ask important questions; they give thoughtful analyses and find enjoyment in the work of reading and writing. They reflect genuinely about themselves in relation to the texts and the world.

The samples here come from students ranging from sixth to twelfth grade, and the texts referred to include poetry, epics, novels, speeches, memoir, nonfiction, drama, short stories, and art. I have collected these samples from my own high school classroom as well as from middle school colleagues whose students write reading responses using this same method. Compiling the examples for this section was nothing short of an emotional experience for me: reading through a myriad of samples, in a range of grade levels and a variety of genres, demonstrated to me again and again that when students are given a structured and safe space to think in, they will connect with texts in a profoundly meaningful way.

You can use the chapters in Part 2 of this book in whatever way is most helpful to you. Read it straight through to experience the full range of RR possibilities. Use the table of contents to jump to samples that would most excite your students—and share them as mentor texts. Or flip to the categories that personally intrigue *you*. However you read this section, you will find repeated features for each RR category, including specific directions for students, an in-depth explanation of the category, and some teaching tips.

Additionally, each student example of an RR has two kinds of annotations: *nudges* (N) and *observations* (O). The nudges are examples of the kinds of questions I might ask to help students extend the thinking in the RR. My hope is that by seeing lots of these examples, you will build a repertoire of strategies for teaching with presence as you interact with your own students. The observations point out important features of students' RRs that will help you better understand the qualities of different kinds of responses.

I've grouped the categories in a way that seems logical to me as an English teacher, with each group revolving around a central motif identified in its title. This felt right to me rather than simply listing all thirty-eight categories in a row. But I don't give students these larger groupings; as described in Part 1, I start the year with the fifteen single categories that I think they can best work with and add categories each quarter. This initial classroom list is culled from categories in the first five groups you'll find in these chapters (The Basics, Parsing the Plot, Going Deeper, Claim and Craft, and Examining Structure). Pick and choose the categories that would engage and benefit your students most, and go from there. My groupings in Part 2 are only meant to help you conceptualize the larger patterns.

These groupings are self-explanatory. The Basics (Chapter 5) are the most popular RR categories, in my experience. Parsing the Plot (Chapter 6) includes categories that focus on plot elements, and the categories in Going Deeper with Inferences (Chapter 7) require more subtle inferences. The Claim and Craft categories (Chapter 8) focus on the authors' main ideas and choices, and the categories in Structure (Chapter 9) ask students to look at the scaffolds that shape texts. The latter groupings, Advanced Connections (Chapter 10) and Literary Theories (Chapter 11), are more challenging. Although middle school examples don't appear in these two groupings, that does not mean middle schoolers couldn't use them; with support, even younger students could succeed with these higher-level lenses. As you read about these more advanced categories, consider your own students and whether or not you think they are within their reach. The final grouping, Responding to Visual

Texts (Chapter 12), contains categories about responding to art as opposed to written text. Though students can respond to art using several of the other categories, such as Tell the Theme or Mind the Mood, these special visual categories give students specific ways to think about art.

As explained in Part 1, the categories themselves are not fixed entities or "right answers." They are only windows into a text, some more accessible or applicable than others in any one moment. They can shift or evolve, over time or within a single text. Every year, I tweak existing categories or create new ones. Let your own creativity, and that of your students, emerge as you try RRs in your own classroom—because it inevitably will! Use this section as a reference, as an inspiration, and as a springboard to imagine what your own students could do.

5

Basic Reading
Response Categories

Give an Opinion

Directions to Students

Tell what you think or feel about a certain part and why. You can react to an aspect of character, plot, theme, language, tone, style—anything in the text. But you must be specific.

Category Description

This is the most commonly selected RR—when students become comfortable thinking for themselves, they love to give their opinions. But by having to turn the impulse of "liking" something or "not liking" it into a full RR, students are compelled to dig deeper and refine their initial gut reactions. They must take a few steps in their thinking, asking themselves, *Why don't I like this part of the text? Is it the character? The plot twist? The writing style?* Then, they must reread the text and locate a line to link to their feeling. By nudging their minds in this way, they improve their comprehension of the text as a whole.

Some students do have specific opinions right from the start—they know exactly how they feel about a certain element or part of the text. In these cases, the consistent practice of finding a line or paragraph as ground zero for their opinion will make them more careful and insightful readers. Often students will have trouble with this—they know how they feel and why they feel it, but pinpointing a line feels limiting. When I ask them which passage they are basing their opinion on, they say, "All of it." They can summarize an entire three pages as evidence, but choosing a specific quote seems daunting.

Student Examples

Give an Opinion for *The Eye of Minds* (James Dashner) by Noelle, Grade 7

N Can you think of a character trait for this quality?

I think it is really sad that Michael doesn't miss his parents. In the book it says, "Between school, the Virtnet, and Helga, he hardly had time to miss them" (location 307). This is depressing. It's like he doesn't even know his parents. Every kid should have the chance to love and bond with his or her parents. Michael is completely fine with not connecting with his. It's almost like he's taking them for granted, which is something no child should ever do because parents are the ones who provide for the children.

N How do you picture this family in daily life?

Give an Opinion for *Tuesdays with Morrie* (Mitch Albom) by Joe, Grade 10

N This RR is definitely an Opinion, but if you wanted to give it another category, what could you say?

I wanted to state my opinion on the quote "Death ends a life, not a relationship" (page 174). I couldn't agree more with this profound aphorism. I do believe in this statement because I think as the memories of a person remain in the living, this allows the relationship to live on. I believe that a relationship is basically two people that have an impact on each other. Even in death, people are going to have an impact on others whether that be lessons they have taught them or the memories they leave behind. I am a firm believer in this because it has happened to me. I still think about my deceased uncle, grandparents, and cousins all the time. What they taught me will always resonate with me. A perfect example of this is when Mitch continues to "chat" with Morrie even after death.

O Joe effectively uses a literary term he learned in class. RRs give students a place to try out the new academic language they are learning.

N What did this look like in the book? How and when did it happen?

Teaching Notes

- In my experience, students have used the Opinion category to examine elements such as characters' choices or traits, plot developments, specific statements made by a character or the narrator, cultural values within the text, the author's writing style, and the applicability or importance of a theme. In the beginning, you may notice students using the Opinion category as a catchall for what they think; as their skills become more nuanced, they will gain confidence in using the other labels.

- You may also find students writing, "It was interesting when . . ." and then proceed to give a five-sentence summary without any substantial original thought. In these cases, push the student to verbalize specifically *why* the moment was interesting: Was she surprised by the character's actions? Intrigued by the description or wording? Excited by the plot turn? You might even tell the student to avoid the word *interesting* in subsequent RRs, in favor of a more specific word. With each RR, students can practice articulating their thoughts, reactions, and understanding more precisely.

Ask a Question

Directions to Students

Write a specific question. This can be a question about something you don't understand in the text, or a larger question (about life, literature, or anything) that the text made you consider. Remember, you must still write five sentences—you can do this by explaining what you understand so far before asking the question, or by trying to answer your question after you ask it.

Category Description

The Question RR is another popular category. In this category, the question itself qualifies as the original thought. Students will write questions not only about confusing moments in the text, but also plot twists, vocabulary, cultural references, and the author's purpose. They might ask questions speculating about what will happen. They may even ask philosophical questions about life or metaphysics. One student, Vinny, once questioned not only the vocabulary in a passage from the *Iliad*, but his understanding of vocabulary in general: "My question is, why am I unfamiliar with the vocabulary? Does it have to do with when it was translated and the words I do not know may be outdated?" In this metacognitive musing, Vinny was able to conceptualize the text in a historical context.

In other RR categories, students must prove a point, in a way—they must put forth an idea and offer some bit of evidence. The Ask a Question category, however, is different. It gives students permission to not know, to wonder, to guess. The fact that this category "counts" as much as every other category communicates the importance of *not knowing* to students. It also sets the stage for interesting and productive discussion.

Student Examples

> **Ask a Question for *The Hobbit* (J. R. R. Tolkien)**
> **by Mohammed, Grade 10**
>
> While reading *The Hobbit*, I wasn't quite sure of why Gandalf kept on disappearing at random moments. In the book, Thorin and the rest of the team was traveling alongside Gandalf, when out of nowhere, he vanished. In fact, it seemed like he was guiding them to a specific area and then disappearing because they could not figure out what to do. For example, the dwarves and Bilbo were riding their horses, and they eventually decided to set up camp for the night and Gandalf disappeared. "Not until then did they notice that Gandalf was missing. So far he had come all the way with them, never saying if he was in the adventure or merely keeping them company for a while" (pg. 67). I think that maybe this was because Gandalf wanted the team to get closer together and know each other better while working as a team to help each other out. I feel like that would be the only logical explanation for this.

> **O** This type of question—a plot question—is most common.

> **O** Mohammed answered his own question.

> **N** Why? What is Gandalf's purpose in the book? How is he an archetypal character?

> ### Ask a Question for *The Maze Runner* (James Dashner)
> ### by Hannah, Grade 7
>
> The situation in the book *The Maze Runner* made me ask myself a question: What if everything that happened in the book happened in real life? What if all of a sudden we found ourselves in a strange place with no memory? How would that make us feel? "That . . . that was the only thing he could remember about his life. He didn't understand how this could be possible. His mind functioned without flaw, trying to calculate his surroundings and predicament" (pg. 1). I would feel scared and worrisome. Also, I would probably get a headache all the time from trying to remember stuff.

O Showing her connection with the book, Hannah asks a series of philosophical questions here instead of a question about plot.

N Explain more about what you think it would be like. Would you recognize your family and friends?

Teaching Notes

- When students link their uncertainties and musings about the text to concrete phrases and lines, they make their questions more incisive—instead of declaring, "I don't get it" or "I don't know" when asked about the text, these students now have very specific topics to bring to a discussion.

- After students reveal their Question RRs in a discussion, their classmates often respond: "I had that question too, but I didn't write about it." Frequently, a Question RR addresses a question the majority of students had, whether they wrote about it or not. Many times, students don't realize they have the same question until they hear a classmate ask it.

- You will probably see that students' own Question RRs are frequently ones that you, as a teacher, would put in a set of comprehension questions if you had made a handout. How much more powerful it is to have students ask the questions of each other.

Make a Connection

Directions to Students

A certain point in the text reminds you of another story, poem, movie, song, or something in real life. How are the two alike? Be specific.

Category Description

Students love writing connections, and I love hearing them; to me, making connections to content we read in class demonstrates not only understanding of the material, but engagement with it. In a discussion, Connection RRs cause reactions like laughter or yelps of "Oh, yeah! I saw that too!" Many times students will make connections to movies or television shows; sometimes, they will make connections to texts we read earlier in the year, or a text they read the year before. Many of their connections would make interesting longer essays, and I'm always sure to point those out.

Students often remark that Connection RRs are their favorites. Based on student discussion and my own experience, I've come to the conclusion readers naturally make connections all the time while reading—our minds can't help but link new information to what we've already seen, heard, or know. However, we usually let the connection slip away as quickly as it came, musing briefly at the fleeting coincidence. By giving students space to explore connections, they learn to search for deeper meanings not only in literature, but in life.

Even in the moments when it doesn't come naturally, finding connections helps students understand what they're reading. Of course, as teachers, we know this—having students yoke new knowledge to prior knowledge is a cornerstone of learning. As one student, Owen, put it: "Relating Gilgamesh to Darth Vader from the Star Wars films helped me to understand Gilgamesh's complicated character and moral development." Connections also reveal arcs of influence over time in literature, art, and culture. Plus, finding connections is enjoyable: Building a larger web of knowledge shapes the foundation of not only intelligence, but an engaged, joyful life. It just feels good to find patterns, to recognize archetypes, to see the infinite interplay of all things.

Student Examples

Make a Connection for
"The River-Merchant's Wife: A Letter" (Li Po)
by Callie, Grade 10

Li Po's poem "The River-Merchant's Wife" reminds me of Taylor Swift's song "Come Back . . . Be Here." Po's poem tells of a young girl who at first resists her marriage, but then learns to love and depend on her husband ("I desired my dust to be mingled with yours / Forever and forever and forever" lines 12–13). So when her husband leaves for business, she feels isolated and old. Likewise, Taylor Swift's song is about how at first she didn't want to be attached to her partner, but she did. So when he left her, it ruined her. She didn't think she would miss him so badly and she wanted him back. Both the poem and the song show longing for a partner that is gone.

> **O** Callie's connecting ancient literature with pop culture shows real engagement.

> **N** Can you point to the lines that show this?

Make a Connection for
"The River-Merchant's Wife: A Letter" (Li Po)
by Alyssa, Grade 10

In the poem the river merchant's wife says, "At 14 I married my lord you" (p. 286). I think that this is so crazy that she's younger than me and she is already married. But in CWS class this year we talked about how in some countries girls get married off very young. Mrs. Morcom told my class that the girls' families trade them off to pay off debts. But in this story it doesn't seem like her dad married her off to pay off a debt. It seems like her dad actually wanted her to like him, and that they think that she would really work out with the river merchant. I also read an article in CWS that many times in an arranged marriage the husband's family beats the girl up, but the river merchant's wife doesn't seem like she is abused or anything. She seems like she actually likes him, and they work good together.

> **O** Students often make connections to other classes, and I am always sure to let their other teachers know!

> **N** How are these two cultures (the one in the poem and the one from CWS class) different?

> **N** Can you point to the lines that show this?

Teaching Notes

- In addition to linking texts to pop culture and other classes, students most often link texts to other texts. One seventh-grade student, Jules, wrote an RR about how both Ponyboy from S. E. Hinton's *The Outsiders* and Michael from James Dashner's *The Eye of Minds* were handed weapons to fight with, but neither could physically harm someone with them. Another student, Chris, wrote about how the case of mistaken identity that led to two brothers killing each other in the Greek myth about Otus and Ephialtes also happened with two brothers in *King Arthur and His Knights of the Round Table*. These kinds of connections help build students' capacities for literary analysis.

- Students will also connect what they're reading to their own lives. Arla, a tenth grader, connected Achilles' leadership skills to the Captains Meetings she attended in school; Hannah related Morrie's disease (from Mitch Albom's *Tuesdays with Morrie*) to her mother's own struggle with cancer. These personal connections imprint stories into students' very beings; conversely, students can place their own experiences in the larger framework of human existence.

- The key to effective Connection RRs is to push students to be specific. The five-sentence minimum helps with this, but you may often find yourself needing to nudge students further. Ask questions such as "How exactly are they similar? What specifically happened? Can you put your finger on a specific character trait [or theme, archetype, feeling, etc.]?" Simply naming a similarity is not enough; students need to take a few steps with the comparison.

- Connection RRs often lead to excellent longer papers. When it's time to write a more in-depth, formal paper, encourage students to see if any Connection RRs could be further explored, researched, and developed. Again, the value will be in supporting parallels with specifics, and some students will need help transforming a Connection RR into a viable thesis with effective support. But the final product will likely be academic papers that students are invested in and enjoy writing.

6

Categories for Parsing the Plot

Character Description

Directions for Students

You notice a detail about a character (what he or she looks like, thinks, says, or does). Why is it important? What trait or other idea does it reveal about that character?

Category Description

Most students are adept at identifying character traits and giving examples by the time they get to middle school. The challenge in writing an RR about a character is to find the specific sentence or paragraph that illustrates the trait. Character RRs sound like opinions, appropriately: labeling a character with a trait requires making inferences, and thus the writer is essentially making a claim. Sometimes, during discussions, students will debate a character's traits, which is always a sign of complex thought. The wonderful part about watching those debates is hearing students using quotes from the text as their evidence.

Student Examples

Character Description for *A Separate Peace* (John Knowles)
by Olivia, Grade 10

O Olivia tied her larger idea from the first two sentences to a specific example.

Although Gene and Finny are made up to be the best of friends, the inner dialogue of Gene suggests a slightly dark yearning to lose himself in Phineas. He always seems to be comparing himself to him and bases most of his personal decisions on what Phineas does or how he reacts. For example, in chapter eight after Phineas has returned to Devon, Gene and Brinker discuss enlisting. After seeing that this thought scares Finny, he immediately decides not to enlist, saying, "Phineas was shocked at the idea of my leaving. In some way he needed me" (108). The fact that Phineas seems to need him is good enough to allow him to make up his mind about staying at school. This brings up the issue of codependency and how it is affecting Gene's individual identity.

N Can you give any other examples of Gene's co-dependence? How is this trait linked to the book's conflict?

Character Description for *The Young Elites* (Marie Lu)
by Isabel, Grade 7

O Many students focus on a moment a character exhibits a new or surprising trait. Sometimes they even label this category Change in Character or Character Growth.

On pg. 17, paragraph 5, Adelina changes forever. "Something snapped inside of me. My lips curled into a smile. A rush of energy, a gathering of blinding light and darkest wind." Before this particular event, Adelina felt powerless and restricted against her father, accepting the mental and physical pain he tormented her with. I think after enduring all of that silently, as well as feeling controlled by her father, Adelina has finally built up enough resentment and fury towards her father that she even grew as a person. No longer the submissive girl she was before, I believe Adelina has transformed into a seeker of vengeance, based on the way she grinned when she was unleashing justice upon her father.

N What is it about the author's description that communicates this?

Teaching Notes

- When you read a Character RR that sounds too easy or shallow, push the student toward more multifaceted thinking by asking him to construct a sentence beginning with *Although*. For example, instead of simply saying, "Lancelot is the bravest knight," a student could try to finish that thought with a contrast: "Although Lancelot is the bravest knight, he . . ." He what? *He was disloyal to Arthur. He was unworthy of the Grail. He could not be trusted.* Use the student's initial thought as a springboard to something more complicated.

- Character RRs can clearly overlap with several other categories and may remain shallow if too unfocused. If you see an RR that seems disorganized, redirect the student to his main point, asking questions such as *What's the strongest trait here?* or *What's the one word you're trying to emphasize?* You might even have the student draw parentheses around the sentences that don't fit, and instruct him to rewrite them, keeping focus on the main idea.

- Character Description RRs also make interesting longer papers, especially once students get past a character's initial or most obvious traits. When you read a Character RR that stumbles upon a sophisticated perception of the character, you might suggest the student circle or star it, to "keep it on the radar" for future discussions and writing.

Spot the Setting

Directions to Students

You notice a part that refers to the place or time of the story or poem. *Why is it important?* How does it relate to the theme, characters, or plot?

Category Description

As with character descriptions, students gain a clear understanding of setting during the early years of elementary school. They know that setting means time and place.

They can find descriptions of it in text. What's new here, though, is that they are asked to view setting as a deliberate choice by an author that serves a larger purpose. They are nudged to ask, "Why this setting, as opposed to another?"

This can be a difficult concept to grasp abstractly, so I usually do a minilesson on the deeper symbolism or purposes of setting early in the year. An easy example is a dark forest—I ask students to brainstorm examples of dark forests in literature and film. We then explore the archetypal symbolism and imagine these stories with brighter, less mysterious settings. Students realize that a happier setting wouldn't work. I tell students: Always question the setting. *What purpose does it serve? How is it symbolic? How does it help the author tell the story?*

Student Examples

Spot the Setting for
The Hunger Games (Suzanne Collins)
by Dilan, Grade 7

The tributes (players) have to wait a week to see the environment they'll be fighting on. Then, in 60 seconds, tributes see the environment and immediately have to know what to do. That's what it feels like for Katniss. Over the last week she's been wondering where she will play the Hunger Games. Then, in 60 seconds it's a lot for her to process what to do. For instance, she says, "We are on a plain, flat, open stitch of ground. A plain of hard packed dirt . . . To my left and back, sparse piney woods. This is where Haymitch would want me to go. Immediately" (pg. 148). This is important because it will be a place where Katniss will have to survive against other tributes. Also, Katniss just figured out that she can use the woods to her advantage in the games. Over a period of time, the woods can make the difference between Katniss living or getting killed.

O Dilan realizes that in this book, setting is more than just where the story happens. Setting actually becomes an important part of the plot.

O By including this sentence with the physical description, Dilan shows he understands that the character's thoughts about the setting are significant.

Spot the Setting for
Miss Peregrine's Home for Peculiar Children (Ransom Riggs)
by Morgan, Grade 10

Jacob takes a trip to the island that his grandfather grew up on. He spots a girl that can create fire with her hands, and when the girl notices that he was watching, she runs away. Jacob chases her all the way across the island bogs and through a portal into the past. This portal takes him to September 3, 1940, which is the day before Miss Peregrine's home was destroyed by a bomb dropped during World War II. The portal not only is set in the past, but it also is stuck in a time loop. Jacob's grandfather sent him a letter "dated September third, 1940, and that was the letter [he] needed to read" (Riggs 46). I feel that this is an important factor in the setting because the Peculiar children live the same day over and over, and they would never think to leave the loop because of how much they enjoy living the way they do.

> O Morgan focuses on time rather than place in this discussion of setting.

> O Morgan pinpointed the detail and quote that support the main structure of the novel.

Teaching Notes

- Students are so accustomed to merely identifying settings and not questioning them or making inferences about them; in the beginning, you may find yourself asking students *But why is this important?* more for this category than any of the others. Students view settings as a given and not one choice among many that an author selected. Encouraging them to imagine alternatives helps them see the bigger work of crafting stories.

- Sometimes students will use quotes not overtly related to the setting, but as the basis for inference. For example, Maddie was able to deduce that *The Handmaid's Tale* (Margaret Atwood) happened in the United States when Offred remembered a scrapbook of her mother's, containing an old bill with "In God We Trust" printed on it. These sophisticated inferences demonstrate the student's active engagement with the text.

Mark the Motivation

Directions to Students

You realize a character's motive (or motives)—what a character *wants*. Explain what this is and how it affects the story or other characters. Why is the motive important?

Category Description

All stories are made up of two ingredients: (1) a character who (2) wants something—something to happen, something to stop, some tangible thing, some intangible thing such as acceptance or love. The motivation may be revealed in the beginning of the story or may not appear until some chapters in. But it is there. Motivation is the engine of the story.

Students understand motivation, and they can understand—sooner or later—how motivation differs from character traits. Consider the exchange between Johnny and Ponyboy from *The Outsiders* (57) just after Johnny killed Bob:

> "You really killed him, huh, Johnny?"
>
> "Yeah." His voice quavered slightly. "I had to. They were drowning you, Pony. They might have killed you. And they had a blade . . . they were gonna beat me up. . . ."

Johnny's motivation for killing Bob was to save his friend and himself. But that's not a character trait; calling Johnny *loyal*, *fearful*, or *shy* would be examples of character traits. Of course, traits and motivation influence each other and overlap in complex ways, but they are not the same. It is exciting to see students realize this. Students will also begin to find subtler motivations within the main character, and motivations within minor characters as well—all of which is evidence of them fine-tuning their skills.

Student Examples

Mark the Motivation for *Hatchet* (Gary Paulsen)
by Will, Grade 10

While Brian is getting wood to make a bow, there is the faint sound of a plane engine overhead. He doesn't notice it until the plane is almost overhead, which causes him to break into a panic and run back to his shelter. When he gets back, he tries to signal the plane but it has already turned and won't be back after that. That night, Brian broke down and almost took his life but in the morning, he woke up and made a decision right then and there that he would not let death win him over, hence being his motivation to keep going. "He was not the same. The plane passing changed him, the disappointment cut him down and made him new . . . he would not die, he would not let death in again" (pg. 46). This specific case of motivation is also intriguing because it seems to be a reoccurring event where people almost take their lives but then decide they actually want to live afterwards.

> **O** Although the main character had been trying to survive for some time, Will finds the moment where the motivation to survive floundered and was reborn from a deeper place.

> **N** You seem to be speculating about an *archetype* here. Where else have you seen this same theme? How was it similar and different?

Mark the Motivation for *Unbroken* (Laura Hillenbrand)
by Bridget, Grade 10

Louie was allowed to make a radio broadcast to his family while he was a prisoner of war. I was stuck wondering why. It seemed like the Japanese had a motive behind letting him do this. I believe that this motivation was that the United States had declared him dead already. Since Louie was never registered into the Red Cross's records, his family was never notified that he was alive. Everyone in the United States was told, out of protocol, that Louie was dead. Louie Zamperini was an Olympian so the Japanese knew that he would create buzz. Louie was just a form of propaganda. I realized this on page 187. After Louie did his first broadcast the Japanese said, "What a lovely voice Louie had . . . How about another broadcast?" I knew at this moment that something else was happening behind the scenes because the Japanese didn't care how Louie sounded; they just wanted him to speak again.

> **O** Bridget detects the motives not of the main character, but of the antagonists in the story. This shows a sophisticated understanding of motive.

> **O** Bridget creates a record of her thinking by detailing her process of questioning and realization: "I was wondering . . ." "I realized . . ." "I knew . . ."

Teaching Notes

- As with other RRs, push students to not only identify the motivation but also to speculate about why these motives exist.

- Beware of generalized answers for this category. Students may be able to easily verbalize an overall motivation that propels the story: survival, acceptance, loneliness, and so on. When they have to tie that idea to a quote, their ideas should automatically become more concrete, but sometimes they may need some guidance. If a student is struggling to find a quote, you might ask, "Where's a specific moment or detail that shows he wants to survive (or be accepted or find love)?"

- As with most categories, Mark the Motivation can be used with nonfiction (as seen previously with *Unbroken*). When students began using this category to explain the *author's* motivation for writing the text, I decided to create a new category, Pinpoint the Purpose (Chapter 8), which gives students more space to specifically focus on an author's purpose. However, students may still sometimes include the author's purpose under Mark the Motivation, especially if the author is also a character.

Detect a Conflict

Directions to Students

You sense a conflict in the story—it can be large or small, external or internal. Describe it, and explain why it is important in the story.

Category Description

After character motivation, the next important ingredient in a story is conflict. The character wants something, but for some reason cannot get it. Conflicts can manifest themselves in many ways, and most stories have layers of conflicts and conflicts that offshoot from other conflicts. Good stories contain internal as well as external conflicts. This path of conflicts that leads to the climax and ultimate resolution makes up the plot. Here, students can choose to focus on any aspect of conflict that strikes them (pun intended!).

When I first included this category, I was afraid students would jump at the easy answers—the largest, most obvious conflicts. But I found that students frequently found subtler conflicts to write about, or internal conflicts, even within minor characters. And of course, even if a student chooses to write about the most obvious conflict in the story, he still must tie it down to a quote and explain its impact.

Student Examples

Detect a Conflict for *Me Before You* (Jojo Moyes) by Olivia, Grade 7

Will has been hurt and is in a wheelchair. But that isn't the whole conflict. Because of Will's accident, he is in a wheelchair always sitting and thinking about his mistakes. Will feels like he doesn't have a future because of his injury. "He'd come pretty far in rehab, but after a year with no improvement I think he found it tough to keep believing it was worth it" (pg. 70). Sadly, Will also tried to kill himself: "Will tried to . . . kill himself" (pg. 102). Will's mother has sadly accepted that if he doesn't get a better outlook on life he will try to kill himself again. He gave his family a time that he would try to feel better and if he didn't he would die.

> O Olivia transitioned from the large, external conflict of the novel to Will's internal conflict.

> N What character traits does this suggest Will might possess?

> O Olivia effectively weaves in a second relevant quote.

Detect a Conflict for *The Epic of Gilgamesh* by Aidan, Grade 10

There was one main conflict in this story: the battle of Gilgamesh and Enkidu vs. the giant Humbaba. This conflict obviously fell to Gilgamesh's favor as they defeated the giant. However, I found a smaller conflict that is also worth noting. At the beginning, I found an internal conflict about how hesitant Enkidu was to go battle the giant. He says, to Gilgamesh, "You have never met him, so you don't know the horror that lurks ahead. But when I saw him, my blood ran cold" (pg. 19). This shows the human side of Enkidu and this could end up being a weakness of either Enkidu for being scared or Gilgamesh for being too comfortable.

> O Aidan moves beyond the main conflict to something more subtle: Enkidu's internal conflict.

> N Could this be a character trait? What's another word for it?

> N What do you predict will happen during the battle?

Teaching Notes

- If a student simply notes the main conflict in the story without going much deeper—"The conflict is that the Greasers and Socs are fighting"—you can check the quote the student used in the RR for a way to nudge her into deeper thought. Ask the student about the people involved in the quote or the scene the quote came from.

- You can also ask the student to connect the conflict to other elements, by asking questions such as *Could this conflict touch upon a theme, and if so, which one?* or *Did this conflict arise from a character trait of the main character? How?* Encourage students in future RRs to always connect the conflict to another element in the text.

Find Foreshadowing

Directions to Students

You read something that seems like a hint to what will come later. Explain why you think this, and make a prediction.

Category Description

In elementary school, we train students to predict what might happen in a story. In middle and high school, the impulse to predict should evolve into the ability to detect foreshadowing. Foreshadowing is a prediction tied to a quote; it is a nod to author's craft.

I stress to students that although their attempts to identify foreshadowing should be grounded in text, it is OK to be incorrect. I don't want to discourage any hunches or intuitions—but I do want students to prove that the text supports their musings. They can be wrong in the end, I tell them, and in fact, authors often intentionally weave red herrings into the story—this sparks class discussions about author's purpose and why readers enjoy some level of the unknown. But as careful readers, students must always be prepared to back up any guesses with text.

Student Examples

Find the Foreshadowing for
The Hunger Games (Suzanne Collins)
by Dilan, Grade 7

"'Well, there's been a change of plans. About our current approach,' says Haymitch. 'Peeta has asked to be coached separately.' . . . Betrayal" (pg. 113, 114). This seems like a hint to come later because for over a week Peeta has been practicing with Katniss. Maybe once he saw Katniss show her strengths and weaknesses he decided that he has enough knowledge to kill her. To Katniss, Peeta feels like a traitor. Katniss is infuriated because these are the things why she didn't want to practice with Peeta in the first place. Later in the book, I feel that Peeta will turn on Katniss and eventually try to kill her.

> **N** Can you think of a character trait for Katniss, based on what you've explained here?

> **N** What word in your quote supports this?

Find the Foreshadowing for
The Eye of Minds (James Dashner)
by Jules, Grade 7

During *The Eye of Minds*, the main character Michael experiences horrible headaches after being attacked by Killsims, dog-like creatures that can kill the gamer's avatar and flesh bodies. During one of these nauseating headaches Michael is spoken to by an unfamiliar voice: "He hoped it had just been the delusion of his attack, but he could've sworn he'd heard a voice, whispering a phrase in his mind. *You're doing well, Michael*" (pg. 153). I believe that in future chapters this mysterious voice will have something to do with the impending antagonist, Kaine. This citing of foreshadowing and prediction is based on The Path, a route created by Kaine for gamers and hackers to find him and his hideout. It is along The Path that Michael hears this mysterious voice and experiences horrible headaches.

> **N** Why would the antagonist be encouraging the main character?

> **O** Foreshadowing often requires students to think about multiple text clues.

Teaching Notes

- Sometimes, students will write Foreshadowing RRs after they've reached the end of a portion of text: once the outcome is discovered, the bread crumbs leading to it become apparent. This type of revelation exemplifies the author's deliberate choices. Encourage students to look back for signs of foreshadowing after a plot twist occurs.

- By middle school, students are usually well trained from books and movies to find foreshadowing. As a minilesson, you could have a whole-class discussion about foreshadowing in a popular movie or in a book most of the students have read.

Clarify the Climax

Directions to Students

You read a part that you realize is the biggest event (or most important moment) in the story. Explain *why* it is so important, and what questions or problems get resolved because of it.

Category Description

Unlike other categories, Clarify the Climax does have a right answer. The climax of a story is a specific moment or event. At first, I hesitated to include this category in my choices because it seemed too straightforward and potentially easy for students. One student, Dani, wrote in her reflection that she never chooses Climax RRs because "many of our readings are philosophical and don't have a very prominent climax. When there is a climax I have trouble expanding on the idea because it is quite straightforward." Many students, especially in high school, may feel this way and prefer to choose more open-ended responses.

However, the ability to not only identify but explicate a climax is a real skill and is not as easy as it looks. Many students mistakenly choose near-climaxes, or even just mildly exciting events, as the climax. And even if students *can* name the climax, more thought is required to explain why it is important and what it resolves in the story. So the category remains on my list of choices, though it is not frequently selected. But if even one student writes a Climax RR and offers it for discussion, the rest of the class can benefit from hearing a reader identify the climax and examine its repercussions.

Student Examples

Clarify the Climax for
The Hunger Games (Suzanne Collins)
by Gray-Paul, Grade 7

> **O** Gray-Paul shows she understands the climax typically resolves something important in the plot.

The climax is when Katniss and Peeta both hold out the nightlock berries. The berries would kill them instantly. They don't eat the berries. The announcer stops them because he needs a winner. It is the climax because it is when the Hunger Games end and Katniss and Peeta are declared winners. "I lift one hand to my mouth, taking one last look at the world. The berries have just passed my lips when the trumpets start to blare" (pg. 345). If they didn't do that, they would have to kill each other. They didn't want to kill each other.

> **O** Considering what might have happened if the climax was different is one way to deepen this kind of response.

Clarify the Climax for
Cyrano de Bergerac (Edmond Rostand)
by Alex, Grade 10

> **O** Alex realizes that more than one event contributes to the climax in this story.

The climax in *Cyrano de Bergerac* was during the part where Christian realized Cyrano was in love with Roxanne, making it clear to him as to why his best friend was so good at wooing her. This is also why Cyrano was so quick to accept the request to write her letters in the first place. Also, another event that contributed to the climax was when Cyrano almost confessed his love for Roxanne, but didn't. In Act Four, Cyrano was just about to tell Roxanne that he was in love with her when Le Bret told him that Christian had been shot. He says, "I can never say it now. Finished . . . Whatever it was doesn't matter now" (Rostand 147). This scene, as sad as it was, was the one that contained the most action and drama, and because it was the point at which the play took a major turn, I considered it to be the climax.

> **N** What is a character trait for Cyrano here?

> **O** I can clearly see Alex's thought process here as she justifies her analysis.

Teaching Notes

- Students frequently choose events in the rising action of the story as climaxes. When this happens, you might say something such as, "This event is definitely important to the story. But does it answer all the story's questions? Do all the problems get resolved here?" If the student can see that problems still linger, he will understand that the event is not the true climax.

- It's OK to let students in on a valuable "secret": Climaxes happen near the very end of stories. If an event occurs and there is still half of the story remaining, it is probably not the climax.

- If a student has correctly identified a climax but the thinking around it is shallow, you might follow up with questions such as:

What problems get resolved at this point?
What would have happened if the climax did not occur?
You've found the exact climax—good. Can you tie it to a theme of the story?
How does this event show one of the messages or lessons of the story?

Encourage students to always think about the climax in the broader context of the work.

Categories for Going Deeper with Inferences

See the Significance

Directions to Students

You realize a certain part in the text is important; you spot a significant passage. Why do you think it's important? What does it mean? What does it tell you about the entire book, story, or poem?

Category Description

Students learn to find "significant passages" in elementary school. But many times, a student will sense a line's importance but be unable to explain why it is important, or the work that it's doing in the larger text. This category does not have the scaffolding of other categories such as Character Description or Spot the Setting. Students must not only detect something significant in the text but also classify it themselves through their explanation.

Like the Opinion category, the Significance category runs the risk of becoming a catchall for generalized thinking. I often find myself pushing students to name the literary element they're trying to explain when they write in this category. Usually, they can do it. Most often, students use this category to discuss a line that relates to a theme; however, significant passages are also commonly about foreshadowing and climaxes. Sometimes students will appropriately focus on a line that is repeated in the text, and try to figure out why it is repeated.

Of course, texts contain plenty of moments, phrases, or descriptions that reveal important information, especially to a discerning reader, but by themselves are not major plot twists or spotlights on themes. Students will sometimes pick up on these significant passages, and this category gives students a space to explore them.

Student Examples

See the Significance for *Walk Two Moons* (Sharon Creech) by Sabrina, Grade 6

"One of the maple leaf circles was mine. The other was Ben's" (pg. 125). This is a very significant passage because this is when the readers realize how much Ben and Sal are alike. When Mr. Birkway asked them to draw their souls for fifteen seconds, both Ben and Sal drew the same thing: a circle with a maple leaf with the ends touching the circle. Sal described that everyone was amazed at what had come from their pencils. No one thought, they just drew. Without thinking, Ben and Sal drew duplicate drawings and received many "Geez!"s and "Wow!"s. At this moment, Sal realized just how similar they were.

> N Does this change Sal's perception of Ben in any way?

> O Sabrina is touching upon the author's craft here—the idea of how and when ideas are revealed in a story.

See the Significance for *Blink* (Malcolm Gladwell) by Ryelee, Grade 10

Near the end of this book, Gladwell is explaining what we need to know to make major improvements in certain tasks. He says, "We can prevent the people fighting wars or staffing emergency rooms or policing the streets from making mistakes" (Gladwell 253). This passage seems important to me because there is so much we don't know, and Gladwell says that if we can control rapid cognition, we will see a decrease in mistakes that people make when under pressure. When we are under extreme stress, we tend to take things too fast. We don't slow down and see what the best solution for the situation is. This often leads to major problems, sometimes fatal. If there was time to slow things down, look at the whole picture, and see what's really going on, our world will seem much easier, and less violent.

> O Strong summary and paraphrasing here.

> N Have you ever personally experienced this?

> O Ryelee effectively pinpoints Gladwell's justification for the main idea in the book.

Teaching Notes

- If a student uses the Significance category to point out something that could be more accurately labeled by another category, you don't need to "correct" it, because many categories overlap. To give the student some practice in being more specific, though, you might say, *What you've identified here is definitely significant. And what else could you call it, in literary terms? Do you think it relates to characterization, or theme, or symbolism . . .*

- If students are reading the same text, it might be fun to ask if anyone else highlighted the same quote found in a student's Significance RR. If others did, ask what labels they used, and why. This will get a discussion going about different ways to consider the same line. What one student called a significant passage, another may have noted for its figurative language or connection to her own life.

Tell the Tone

Directions to Students

You sense the speaker's (author, narrator, or character) attitude as you read. What is it? Why do you think this? What is causing it—the word choice, the meaning of the words, the sentence structure, the genre itself? Explain.

Description of Category

Tone can be difficult to detect and often gets confused with mood. Mood is about how the *scene* feels (frequently related to setting). Tone is about someone's *attitude*.

Students definitely understand the difference between the meaning of someone's words versus the meaning of someone's voice as the words are spoken—that is, the difference between *what* is said versus *how* it is said. They know what it means when a friend sarcastically says, "Oh, I had a *great* time!" and means the exact opposite; they know what parents mean when they say, "Don't you take that tone with me!"

Even in digital media, we employ emojis to communicate tone. Think of a message with an eye roll emoji after it, versus a message with the blushing emoji. Or the LOL emoji versus the angry emoji. These communicate tone and intent, albeit in a less sophisticated way than our actual voices can.

So students get it. It becomes a bit trickier, however, when they have to find tone in a well-crafted piece of nonfiction or fiction, without the ability to hear someone's voice. And authors don't usually include emojis in the margins of their work! Students must rely on other cues, such as word choice and meaning.

Whose tone is conveyed in a work is also sometimes confusing. The only time readers can be sure that the tone they are reading is the author's is in a piece of nonfiction that is clearly voiced by its author, such as an op-ed piece, letter, speech, or autobiography. The speaker in a poem is not necessarily the author, and narrators in fiction are obviously not the authors. Even memoir can tread into a grey area. With Tell the Tone, students may focus on an author, narrator, or character's voice, but they should try to identify the voice in their responses.

Student Examples

N How do the sentence lengths in the passage you've chosen contribute to this tone?

N Which word choices (that you mention at the end) contribute to this? Think about the difference between *killed* and *murdered*, for example.

Tell the Tone for "Chief Joseph Surrenders"
by Katie, Grade 11

"I am tired of fighting. Our Chiefs are killed. Looking Glass is dead, Tu-hul-hil-sote. The old men are all dead." The tone in Chief Joseph's speech is very somber and tired. His people are being killed and their sacred ground is being pillaged by the government so they could cultivate more land for national parks or for other selfish gains. He is telling the government peacefully that he doesn't want to fight and that his people were told they wouldn't have to fight when they first made an alliance with Lewis and Clark. He is tired of losing the family that he has because they keep getting pushed out further and further away from their home. They are getting pushed into areas where they cannot survive: "The little children are freezing to death." He talks about how the white man would often commit actions like this in the past but the Nez Percé have always looked passed it because they always wanted to keep the peace. Now that all of their family is dying, Chief Joseph is telling them that he is tired and will no longer be silent. Although he is taking a stand, his tone is never angry; he's simply stating what he wants from the white men in the future. Overall, the speech is very sad and the reader is able to feel the Chief's hopelessness through his word choice and examples.

O The text example Katie includes ("little children freezing to death") shows she's really attending to the power of specific detail.

Tell the Tone for
The Paris Architect (Charles Belfoure)
by Olivia, Grade 10

Throughout the novel *The Paris Architect* I read many gruesome scenes of torture. Although these were twisted to read, they were very crucial to the plot of the story, because this is what happened to real people during the actual German Occupation. I noticed that in every interrogation and torture scene, the author gave the German officers a sarcastic tone. Although this seems like a minor detail I feel that it was crucial to building the characters of these men. An example of this is when the officers are interrogating a carpenter. "'What would happen if you didn't have your index finger? Make it hard to cut wood, maybe?' Voss snipped off Aubert's entire right index finger as if it were the stem of a flower" (pg. 305). The dialogue before the violence shows this sarcastic tone. I feel that the sarcastic tone really shows how evil and twisted these characters are. They make the pain of other men sound like a joking matter. It's crazy how important the tone that the author uses is when developing a character.

> **O** Olivia ties tone to author's craft and purpose.

> **O** Olivia's close reading of the passage illuminates the cruelty of the torturers.

> **O** Olivia realizes that tone is a subtle but important building block of character development.

Teaching Notes

- If students are struggling to understand tone, here's a fun minilesson you might try. Give a group of students the same sentence, such as, "A clown is approaching the door." Then give each student a card with a different tone on it, such as *joyful*, *angry*, *fearful*, *sarcastic*, and *nervous*. Ask each student to say the sentence in his or her prescribed tone, then discuss how tone creates meaning.

- You might also gather some tone-driven texts—letters to the editor, perhaps, or snippets of speeches—and have students draw emojis in the margins as the tone of the author fluctuates. This amusing visual exercise will help students depict the feelings behind the words.

Mind the Mood

Directions to Students

You feel the mood of the piece. What is it, and what is creating it? (Something in the setting? Dialogue? Plot? Sensory details?) Remember that mood is the feeling in the text, not the author's attitude. Your quote should show evidence of the mood. Then: Why is the author doing this?

Category Description

If tone is about a speaker's feeling behind his or her words, mood is about the feeling behind a scene in general. Mood is the feeling you get when a movie begins and creepy music plays; mood is the feeling that washes over you when looking at a painting of a deep-orange sunset on a quiet beach. In a text, however, there is no music playing or paintings projected into air; there are only words. Mood, then, is the feeling created by the imagery and description in a passage. Most often, mood comes from setting, but it can come from the action as well.

I sometimes give students this scenario: Picture a scary scene in a scary movie, where the crazy, hockey-masked killer is approaching a deserted barn, in which two about-to-be victims are hiding for their lives. One of them whispers, "Should we scream for help?" The friend says, "Sure, let's send him an invitation right to our hiding spot." The tone of the friend is sarcastic. But the mood of the scene is suspenseful, scary, and tense. Other scenarios can work as well. In a sad, wrenching hospital scene, for example, someone can say something humorous (or kind, or mean). How they speak is tone; how the scene feels is mood.

As always, students must also tie their inference about mood to a quote. This is especially important because often readers can feel the mood while reading, but struggle to put a finger on what, exactly, is creating it. Investigating the specifics that create a mood can lead to rich discussions about author's craft and style.

Student Examples

Mind the Mood for the *Iliad* (Homer)
by Keena, Grade 10

The mood from Book 1 is very hostile and angry. What makes the text so angry and hostile is an argument between Agamemnon and Achilles. Now, we already know that both men hate each other with a burning passion, which only adds to the piece. The argument between Agamemnon and Achilles is about Agamemnon returning the priest's daughter and then claiming Achilles' prize, Briseis. In the story Agamemnon says, "You—I hate you most of all the warlords" (pg 371). Achilles then responded to Agamemnon by drawing his sword. It wasn't until the Goddesses Hera and Athena intervened and stopped the two enemies from acting so childish. But even after the goddesses left they continued to argue but no swords were drawn because they would not dare go against the words of the goddesses.

> N So what exactly creates the mood? Can you categorize the evidence that you give with literary terms?

> N Why do you think this? What is the deeper issue at stake for these two men?

Mind the Mood for
"next to of course god america i" (e. e. cummings)
by Emily, Grade 12

The mood of "next to of course god america i" by e. e. cummings is rushed, as if the speaker is attempting to get out the words before they are halted. This mood is set by the form of the poem, the fragmented sentences that branch off randomly. The open-ended references to iconic American songs are half finished to depict the open-ended, rushed mood. There's little punctuation, which adds to the hurried sense of the piece—so hurried the narrator cannot finish his sentence, or pause for a breath. The last sentence, "He spoke. And drank rapidly a glass of water" (line 14), implies him flushing out his words with water, as if he was afraid to say them.

> O Emily effectively identifies the mood, as opposed to the tone (which is cynical or critical).

> N What do you think the speaker could be afraid of? Could this be related to the theme?

Teaching Notes

- Depending on your students' previous experience in identifying and discussing mood, you may need to plan some teaching that shows them how to link moods to text. You might simply examine sample texts together and discuss mood, but visuals can also help. Show students pictures or videos of scary scenes, tense moments, or joyful victories, and then ask, *What feeling does this picture create? Why? How? What do you see that contributes to the feeling?* List the details students offer, and then attach the details to literary elements such as setting, dialogue, or sensory details.

- Another way to explore this idea is to give your students a mood, such as "joyful," and have them list all the things in the classroom that would contribute to that mood if you were writing it into a story. Answers usually include any bright clothing, inviting decorations, sunny weather, or smiling faces. Then, give them another mood like "boring" or "depressing." Answers may include the drab green chalkboard, gray sweatshirts, bare trees through the window, or worn tiles on the floor. Help them see that, in any moment, thousands of details exist; writers choose the ones that serve the mood. This activity can even be assigned as a "field experience" exercise to be done out of school.

- Unlike the Conflict category, identifying the mood will never be too obvious. But tying the mood to a quote in the text might prove difficult. Always direct students to the most concrete details they can find.

Theme Recognition

Directions to Students

You find a sentence or two that might connect to a theme (the message or "So what?") of the piece. Explain the theme, and explain how that portion of text relates to it.

Category Description

As with many other categories, by middle school students usually have a basic understanding of theme. Some will say it is the "lesson" of the text; others the "message." I like to share Nancie Atwell's (1998) definition: Theme is the "So what?" of the piece. A story involves a character who wants something (motivation) and who struggles to get it (conflict). Eventually the conflict is resolved. The story may contain beautiful language. But after all is said (via the language) and done (via the plot), so what? Why should readers bother to read it? What can readers take away from the text? The answer to these questions is the theme.

Authors work hard to develop themes. They build them meticulously into the story, weaving plot, character, and narration together to form coherent messages. The one-word summaries we give to overall themes—ideas such as "survival" or "growing up"—are subtly nuanced and layered in a well-written text. For this reason, asking students to find evidence of a theme in an actual line or two for their RRs may prove challenging. But they have five sentences—and more—to explain their ideas, so they should be able to connect the dots of their thinking.

Student Examples

Theme Recognition for
Into the Wild (Jon Krakauer)
by Conor, Grade 10

"We like companionship, see, but we can't stand to be around people for very long. So we go get ourselves lost, come back for a while, then get the hell out again" (pg 67). This conveys the main theme of this entire book. This is the need for human interaction vs the need for people to be alone. Throughout the book, the author talks about people that have a similar story to the one of Chris McCandless. In every single story the author describes how this reoccurs in every person. That person loves being around people for a certain amount of time. Then out of nowhere they stop enjoying it then go back out into the wild. After a while with no human contact they start craving it again. It's a cycle in every single story and it tells the theme of this book.

[O] Conor does not try to take a side here; he realizes the theme is the struggle between these two needs. This reflects a sophisticated understanding.

[O] Conor has touched upon author's craft and purpose by noticing the repetition of the theme in different stories throughout the text.

O In the previous RR, Conor found a sentence that stated the theme directly; here, Krutik effectively illustrates the theme with events.

Theme Recognition for "The Story of Daedalus and Icarus" by Krutik, Grade 10

In "The Story of Daedalus and Icarus," Daedalus (dad) makes wings for his son (Icarus) and instructs him to not go too high nor too low. The father instructs the son very carefully but Icarus got lost in what he was doing. During the flight he becomes overconfident and flies too high and the wax on the wings melts and he falls down into the water. "And the boy thought *This is wonderful!* and left his father, soared higher, higher, drawn to the vast heaven, nearer the sun, and the wax that held the wings melted in the fierce heat . . . until the blue sea hushed him" (lines 48–55). He becomes too overconfident and falls into the sea. The moral of the story is that overconfidence could result in critical consequences.

N Can you think of other stories that have this theme?

Teaching Notes

- Students sometimes get creative about the quotes they choose to support a theme. In an RR for Sharon Creech's *Walk Two Moons*, Sabrina (grade 6) used the quote "It's a vase. Obviously" (207) to illustrate the theme of people's differing perspectives. The quote refers to the characters' opposing interpretations of the famous "vase or faces" drawing. Encourage students to be on the lookout for sentences that state the theme outright, but also to not be afraid to look for themes buried in smaller events or dialogue.

- Be sure to remind students that themes can be unresolved, as in Conor's example. An RR about an unresolved theme can turn into a discussion of author's purpose: often, authors do not want to "teach" a specific lesson. The theme is more subtle than didactic.

Sensing a Symbol

Directions to Students

You notice an object or detail (in nature or human-made) that seems to mean something deeper. What is it and what is it doing? Have you seen it before in the text? What could it mean? What theme or character could it point to? Why do you think this?

Category Description

When a well-wrought symbol appears in a crucial moment of a text, the passage takes on a three-dimensional quality, with layers of meaning infusing the scene. Think of roses, the stars, the seasons, the moon, or water of any kind. Think of Wordsworth's (and Genesis') rainbow, Bronte's moors, Coleridge's albatross, Frost's roads, or the color red in Hawthorne's *Scarlet Letter* or Atwood's *Handmaid's Tale*. Symbols abound.

Symbols are so prevalent that many have become archetypes, and in our modern day can border on the clichéd. Contemporary authors must use them wisely, and they do. Examples include Harry Potter's lightning bolt or Esperanza's experiences with shoes throughout *The House on Mango Street*. Symbols can turn up as an actual part of the plot or setting or wrapped in a simile or metaphor. Used meaningfully, symbols reflect the author's craft.

People enjoy recognizing symbols because they feel like they're in on the author's secret messaging, but it takes practice to be able to engage with a story while simultaneously thinking about how it's crafted. We can help students cultivate the habit of looking for symbols. They should look closely at details such as objects, landscapes, weather, and sounds, and question everything. Keep reminding students to ask themselves, *Does it mean something deeper?* At the end of the year in my class, we watch parts of *Troy*; it has so many perfectly placed crow caws that students laugh about it. "Someone's about to die," they groan. That's exactly how I want them to feel: smart; vigilant; versed in archetypes. I want them to believe that finding symbols is a skill that can be acquired, like any another ability.

Student Examples

Sensing a Symbol for *Walk Two Moons* (Sharon Creech) by Sabrina, Grade 6

> N What do you think the author means by this word?

"She kept climbing and climbing. It was a thumpingly tall ladder. She couldn't see me, and she just never came down. She just kept going" (p. 162). In this chapter Sal has a dream where her mother is climbing a ladder. She doesn't come down or even look at Sal. She just keeps climbing. This is symbolic of Sal's mom leaving and not coming back. This idea is the main conflict that the whole book is about. We don't know what happened to Sal's mom right now but the main conflict must be solved.

> O Sabina insightfully ties symbol to conflict.

> N Do you think Sal herself realizes this?

Sensing a Symbol for the *Iliad* (Homer) by Maddie, Grade 10

In Book 16, I feel like Achilles's spear has a deeper meaning. The text says, "But he [Patroclus] did not pick up the famous spear of Achilles . . . Achilles alone could use it. It was made of ash . . . as a gift to Achilles's father" (147). When I first read this, I didn't think much of it. However when you think about it, the spear could be a symbol for Achilles's honor and power. While there may be other successful fighters, no one can match Achilles's strength and power, just like how no one can use his spear. He is the best of the best and everyone knows it.

> O The process of writing the RR has caused Maddie to deepen her thinking about the text.

> O Maddie makes this conclusion based on the word *famous* in the quote above. This demonstrates a close, careful reading of the text.

Teaching Notes

- Books are often titled after their most significant symbols. In Symbol RRs that could just as easily be labeled Title RRs, Alex (grade 10) wrote an RR about Sylvia Plath's bell jar and Will (grade 10) wrote about the importance of Gary Paulsen's hatchet.

- Just as often, symbols are more subtle. Achilles' ash spear is not a title or even a significant part of the plot in Book 16, though it is an important symbol. Similarly, many students who read *Tuesdays with Morrie* note that Morrie's windowsill flower is an important symbol of the impermanence of life.

- Dreams almost always contain symbols, so make sure students know that if a character is dreaming, the author is offering some clues.

- Films employ symbolism extensively. Ask students for symbols they've noticed in their favorite films. Create a list of each object and its deeper meaning.

Clarify a Cultural Value

Directions to Students

You notice that a certain event, detail, message, or character trait reveals a specific value of that culture. What is it? How do you know it's a value? Explain, and make sure your quote supports your idea.

Category Description

Students will often notice details that seem "different" from their daily lives, especially when reading historical fiction, but they become so immersed in their stories that they don't stop to process these differences. Many times in class I will ask something like, "Did you realize that children used to work instead of going to school in those days?" Students will nod and usually one remarks, "Oh, yeah, I thought that when I was reading." With this category, I want to give students a space to think about those differences and the deeper value they represent.

The idea of "different cultures" could mean several things. It obviously points to different countries or ethnicities, but it also could be applied to different eras, even in a student's own culture. Cultural values are rarely spelled out; authors simply write using the cultural values of the time and place of the story. Futuristic stories may have cultural values invented by the author. But most values must be inferred by the characters' actions and thinking. The importance of having students look deeply into how a culture can influence a character cannot be underestimated. Understanding that people do things differently because they value different ideas is a skill that will help students grow—as professionals and persons—in our increasingly global world.

Student Examples

> ### Clarify a Cultural Value for "Pericles' Funeral Oration" by Keena, Grade 10
>
> While reading "Pericles' Funeral Oration," I noticed a common idea we saw in the *Iliad*: honor. In this piece, honor is a very important value, especially if you die for your country. Peace, honor, democracy, and dying for your country are the best things achievable. When a soldier dies, their families are comforted by the thought of the glory their late family member had earned protecting his country. In the text, it says, "In the fighting, they thought it more honorable to stand their ground and suffer death than to give in and save their lives" (p. 430). This means they would rather die protecting their country than to protect themselves—the greatest glory. This is what we saw with Hector in the *Iliad*, he would rather die by the hands of Achilles than to suffer from being a coward.

N Do we have this same cultural value today?

N Do you think this helped the families?

O Wonderful connection with another in-class text. A semicolon would solve the run-on.

> **O** I think Katya realizes this, but I would emphasize that this was the ancient Chinese and not the contemporary culture.

Clarify a Cultural Value for "The River-Merchant's Wife" (Li Po) by Katya, Grade 10

From this passage, I can tell that the Chinese married their children off young and didn't do it for love. It's pretty evident how young the Chinese were willing to give up their daughters from "At fourteen I married" (Pound 286). I know that in other societies children were married off as young as thirteen or fourteen, but it still shocked me a little. Then I could tell that she didn't particularly care for her husband at first when she says, "I looked at the wall. / Called to, a thousand times, I never looked back" (Pound 286). Her husband is the one calling her, but she continues to stare at the wall because she is shy and would probably rather be with her birth family. Then, she develops an attachment to her husband by fifteen when she "desired [her] dust to be mingled with [his]/forever and forever and forever" (Pound 286). She eventually learned to care about her spouse, but we can tell the Chinese did not marry their children for attachment to each other.

> **N** Why do you think they did it? Can you see any reasons why this culture would participate in this practice?

> **O** Excellent blending of quotes throughout.

Teaching Notes

- You might introduce the idea of cultures to students by pointing out that each of them belongs to several mini cultures—the field hockey team, the school cafeteria, their family, the school choir—and each of these is its own culture with its own "rules" and values. Have students make a Code of Chivalry for a group or space they belong to. Students will enjoy making Codes of Chivalry for the soccer field, or the movies, or Snapchat. This will show them that even small, everyday events are governed by norms that must be learned.

- Point out cultural values in texts whenever possible. Texts about different historical times, different countries or regions, or even different ethnic groups will have cultural values that diverge from what students know. Then, always ask the follow-up question: *Do we have this cultural value today, here?*

Categories for Exploring Claim and Craft

Pinpoint the Purpose

Directions to Students

You begin to realize the author's reason for writing the text; you sense the author's intention behind it all. Perhaps the author is trying to persuade, entertain, or instruct the audience; perhaps it is a combination of intentions. Maybe the author wants readers to wrestle with certain questions and doesn't give a clear answer. Whatever you think, make sure your quote supports your view.

Category Description

Certainly, the idea of author's purpose is a staple in English classes from elementary through high school. Ideas about it appear throughout the Common Core State Standards and on virtually every standardized test imaginable. The idea felt so educationally skill related to me (as opposed to a natural response students would choose) that for a long time, I didn't include it as a category. However, I began to notice students using the Mark the Motivation category as a space to discuss the motivation of the speaker in autobiographical pieces or speeches—hence, the author. The motivation of the author in these cases *is* the author's purpose. I added the category to the list so students would view an author's purpose as something different than the motivation of a main character, even though the author may be the main character in a piece of nonfiction.

Of course, this does not mean students couldn't use this category for fiction or poetry as well. In these cases, students will discuss how the author wanted to explore a theme or send a message or simply entertain readers. Whatever angle students choose, they must still tie the larger purpose to a quote. Perhaps a humorous passage is cited to prove the author's intent to entertain; perhaps a thematic passage demonstrates the intent to challenge readers. By grounding the author's larger purpose with a single sentence or two, students learn to see how big intentions manifest themselves concretely in text.

Student Examples

> ### Pinpoint the Purpose for
> ### "Pericles' Funeral Oration"
> ### by Clay, Grade 10
>
> Pericles is giving this speech at the funeral to the families of the dead warriors from battle. It is a persuasive speech to make the families of the dead feel like their children didn't die in vain. One of his most persuasive lines was, "Their memory abides and grows. It is for you to try to be like them. Make up your minds that happiness depends on being free, and freedom depends on being courageous" (pg. 430). Pericles says all of this to make the families feel like their children were the reason that peace was able to be reached since the warriors went to war to fight against the terror of the enemies and provide safe shelter for their friends and loved ones.

N What are the cultural values inherent in these lines? Do we have these same values today?

O Clay ties his quote to his idea of Pericles' purpose.

O This statement about people in general is a good choice to support Cameron's claim that the author's purpose is "to share vital life lessons."

N Are you sure this is a novel? How do you know?

Pinpoint the Purpose in
Tuesdays with Morrie (Mitch Albom)
by Cameron, Grade 10

In *Tuesdays with Morrie*, the author and narrator, Mitch Albom, has a clear purpose for writing the novel. Mitch finds himself in a point in his life where he is completely caught up in work and not enjoying life as much as he should be. He happens to begin meeting with his old college sociology professor at the same time to which he learns a myriad of life lessons. Morrie says in the story, "So many people walk around with a meaningless life. They seem half-asleep, even when they're busy doing things they think are important" (pg. 13). This resonates with Mitch so much because he is unhappy with the condition of his life. He writes the novel to share the vital life lessons that Morrie imparts upon him to the rest of the world so that they may change the way they live. His overall motivation is to make a positive change in other people's lives.

N Can you categorize the purpose even more concisely? Does Albom want to instruct? Challenge? Help? Entertain? Motivate?

Teaching Notes

● Characters have motivations for their actions, but the author has a main purpose or two for writing the entire text. To help students see the difference between character motivation and author purpose in fiction, you might give students a chart about a book they have all read, focusing on two or three main characters and an action for each:

The Difference Between Character Motivation and Author's Purpose

Characters	Actions	Motivations

On the second half of the sheet, ask who the *author* of the work is. Beneath that, you could have a chart like this:

Author's Name	Author's Possible Purpose	How do you know?

You may have to suggest some possible purposes for students to choose from, and they don't need a long list here—usually about two purposes will suffice. The "How Do You Know?" column will force students to think of scenes or moments in the text that persuade, entertain, instruct, or pose questions. Having it all on one page will help them distinguish between character motivation and author's purpose.

Cite the Claim

Directions to Students

You find a sentence or passage you think is the author's main thesis or claim. Explain why you think it is the central claim of the piece.

Category Description

In this category, students must ask themselves what the author's main claim is. I originally created this category for students to use with shorter, nonfiction pieces, such as op-eds, and for other conspicuously persuasive pieces, such as speeches. To my surprise and delight, however, students use this category just as often to find claims where I would not have thought to look for them: in poems, novels, or soliloquies. As it turns out, persuasion is everywhere, and as long as students can support their idea with a relevant quote and some reasoning, I applaud their efforts.

Identifying a claim differs from identifying the author's purpose: a claim is the idea the author wants the reader to support, and if there is a claim, the purpose is to persuade. But all texts, of course, are not persuasive; some exist only to entertain or to educate without intending for the reader to subscribe to a particular belief. A persuasive text has a specific idea—a claim—that it supports with reasoning and examples. Having students pinpoint a claim will help them better understand how persuasive texts are organized and executed.

Student Examples

Cite the Claim for Malala Yousafzai's speech at the Youth Takeover of the United Nations
by Alie, Grade 8

The claim in Malala's speech is "We will speak for our rights and we will bring change through our voice," in the fifth paragraph from the bottom. Throughout the speech Malala talks about speaking for human rights and raising our voices for ourselves and for others. She also mentions after the Taliban shot her they wanted to silence her, but "out of the silence came thousands of voices." The main message in the speech is that words are stronger than violence. The claim supports this message because it talks about bringing change not through violence, but though our voice. Even Malala making the speech in the first place shows how she will "speak for her rights and bring change through her voice."

N What are some specific examples of rights that Malala names in the speech?

O Alie links the genre to the claim.

> **N** Can you state these as a persuasive claim?

Cite the Claim for "The Guest House" (Rumi)
by Tamane, Grade 10

In Rumi's "The Guest House," he illustrates the human emotions and experiences we go through, and focuses on his main philosophy of being grateful of life and to enjoy it to its fullest extent. He states "The dark thought, the shame, the malice, meet them at the door laughing, and invite them in" (Rumi 122), claiming to meet all of life's dark side with a grin. He advises his audience to greet every human emotion and experience with appreciation and happiness, and to enjoy its presence throughout life, therefore life all together. I believe this outlook on life displays a very hard, although rewarding, way of living life. It is hard sometimes not to think of the soul-crushing mediocrity of the world, and sometimes self-deprecating comments in the mind, causing a pandemonium of spiraling thoughts that plague the conscious. Although this is the case, improvement can be made by being appreciative of life, and all of the components that come with it.

> **N** This quote is a good example of the actions Rumi wants the reader to take. Can you also pinpoint the exact lines that capture the claim?

Teaching Notes

- As these examples show, students find claims in unexpected places. Their responses have made me realize how persuasive poetry can be—something I had not fully considered before. The ability to recognize a persuasive text, or to detect the moment a text becomes persuasive, is a real-world skill that will help students both inside and outside the classroom.

- Students may quote a line that contributes to the claim, but is not exactly the claim, as Tamane did. This is not necessarily incorrect, especially if the student explains the claim in her own words throughout the RR. You can use the opportunity to help the student pinpoint a sentence that more clearly expresses the claim. Identifying the exact claim can give students a sense of what the main idea is and how the supporting ideas are organized around it.

Seeing the Sentences

Directions to Students

You notice a sentence (or group of sentences) and something about the structure seems intentionally crafted. Maybe the sentence is longer or shorter, uses parallelism, or is purposefully a fragment. Maybe something else. What is it that you've noticed, and why do you think the author crafted it this way?

Category Description

The goal of this category is for students to focus intently on the structure or craft of specific sentences, but I've learned through trial and error that this can be a challenge. Students choose the category often, but they frequently treat it as another version of Seeing the Significance; they write about a sentence that is meaningful for its content rather structure. I thought about scrapping the category from my list, but enough students have used it as intended, with insight and fearlessness, that I can't bring myself to delete it. And, of course, even students who write about the content of a sentence rather than its structure are still writing meaningful RRs. So the category remains as a special challenge for any who would accept it.

When students do specifically consider the structure of sentences in an RR, they might label their responses as Language Recognition or Connecting Form and Content as these categories all overlap. When I see this, I remember that the categories are meant to be doorways; whether a student enters through the front door or side door is irrelevant, as long as they're in the house. Showing them several doors only increases their chance of success.

Student Examples

Seeing the Sentences for *Shiver* (Maggie Stiefvater)
by Destiny, Grade 10

Within the monologue on page 352, she states, "I've tried so hard. I never get into trouble. I always do my homework." She says several small sentences, which make the text seem a bit rushed. The reader begins to read faster and the author does this for a reason. Because the reading seems rushed, it shows her frustration and how fast she would be talking if we were listening to her. It's so clever how authors do this to help change the overall mood. While reading, the reader can conclude that Grace is frustrated and angry.

> **O** Destiny is appreciating the author's craft!

> **O** Destiny connects sentence structure to how the character is feeling, and then, to the mood of the scene—she takes several steps here.

Seeing the Sentences for "I, Too" (Langston Hughes)
by Bella, Grade 12

"They'll see how beautiful I am / and be ashamed— / I, too, am America" (lines 16–18). The dashes after "ashamed" emphasize the word, creating a feeling of renewal. The people who said the speaker was not beautiful will now feel the opposite. This poem speaks about racism, the speaker stating he is the "darker brother" (line 2). The fact that "I, too, am America" is its own stanza creates a feeling of pride the speaker is America; they are part of the country, no matter and those who disagree. It is separate because this statement is the theme of the poem. America includes everyone. Everyone in America makes up the country, and everyone in this country is beautiful.

> **O** Bella focuses on a single dash and its effect. This category gives students space to think about these seemingly small choices of authors.

> **N** Are there any other meaningful line breaks or stanza breaks in the poem?

Teaching Notes

● While reading for content, students must also be able to step back and read for craft. With very experienced readers, this may happen simultaneously; less advanced readers may have to reread a text multiple times to see both content and craft. Showing examples of effective RRs in this category can help students see more in texts, as does studying some texts together as a whole class, noting and discussing the craft you see.

- Sometimes, students may notice a sentence structure that seems to serves a meaningful purpose throughout an entire text. For example, Oliviah (grade 10) realized that many of the sentences in *The Handmaid's Tale* are choppy, and she speculated about Atwood's purpose: "In this male-dominated society, there are strict rules, and if one goes off the path in any way, she is severely punished through torture or death. These short sentences could be another way of communicating that rigidness and strictness that has entwined itself into all aspects of the women's lives." Similarly, sometimes students will notice that certain characters speak or think in certain sentence structures. Noting any connection between sentence structure and meaning can lead to illuminating discussions in class.

- As with other categories, there is no need to correct a student who has not fully understood the category's purpose. Instead, ask questions that lead him to think more specifically about the structure of the sentences he's cited: *Do you notice anything about how these sentences are written?* or *This sentence seems short. Does that seem different to you?*

Language Recognition

Directions to Students

You notice some engaging sensory details, a simile or metaphor, some onomatopoeia or alliteration, some parallelism, an interesting epithet, or something else. Maybe you notice a single word and wonder about why the author chose it. Whatever you notice, quote it, and explain how it adds to the text. Does it contribute to the mood or characterization? Does it relate to a theme? Could it have a deeper meaning? What would that be?

Category Description

With this category, students might consider a range of literary techniques—anything from conspicuous similes to the subtle use of sound or an interesting word choice. Identifying these may not be so difficult, but I want students to pause and really think about them. Readers often have fleeting thoughts where they vaguely appreciate vivid description or nice wording. This category gives students space to linger there, to examine the craft and purpose of the language, even if it's just over a short phrase or a single word.

For that reason, the Language Recognition category may feel less intimidating than others: examining a few words from a single sentence will suffice. It does not ask students to write an entire paper about the use and symbolism of an extended metaphor or the deeper meaning of the variations in imagery throughout a longer text. The category asks students to consider only a particular instance of language.

At the same time, it's not enough to say, "This sentence contains a simile." Students must look deeply into the language and say something else about it. Maybe it contributes to the mood or to a character's personality; maybe it even propels the plot in some way. Maybe, as in some cases of repetition, the language contributes to a theme. Whatever it may be, I want students to look for something bigger. More often than not, by the fifth sentence of the RR, the student has stumbled upon a theme or character trait.

One of the reasons I love this category is that it is automatically differentiated. A higher-level student can write about the symbolic meaning of the assonance throughout a poem, for example, and a lower-level student can write about the visualization and importance of a certain simile in a specific line. Both responses fulfill the intentions of the Language Recognition category.

Student Examples

Language Recognition for
The Underground Railroad (Colson Whitehead)
by Ryan, Grade 10

At one point, following the slave masters forcing the slaves to perform a dance for them, a beating ensues. The cause is a bumping of elbows of the slave master and a slave performer. The slave, named Chester, is violently being beaten. Instinctively, another slave, Cora, jumps on top of the small boy to protect him from the beating. The author describes it as, "She was bent over the boy's body as a shield . . . The silver wolf bared its silver teeth . . . the cane was out of her hand. It

> **O** Ryan effectively summarizes the scene in the first four sentences here.

N Can you name exactly what kind of figurative language is used in the quote, besides sensory detail?

O Ryan is touching upon tone and even author's purpose here.

came down on her head. It crashed down again and this time the silver teeth ripped across her eyes and her blood splattered the dirt" (60). In this quote, the reader can sense the author's pity for Cora and the boy just by his words. This is an excellent example of the author using figurative language and sensory details to convey emotions.

O Isabel finds character traits within the sensory detail and description.

Language Recognition for
The Young Elites (Marie Lu)
by Isabel, Grade 7

I think the description of Gemma's laugh is a beautiful description that gives powerful insight to her character. On page 185, paragraph 6, the laugh is described as "a bright ringing sound, the laugh of someone who's loved." The sound of the laugh suggests to me that Gemma is an optimist, as well as surrounded by friends and family. Also, the amazing personality expressed in this laugh is probably going to draw Adelina and her closer. As well as this, the wording in this description was so well done, one could almost hear the laughter for themselves. Gemma could be well analyzed by her marvelous giggle.

O Isabel turns her character analysis into foreshadowing.

Teaching Notes

- Depending on the experience of your students, it might be helpful to conduct minilessons where you define various elements of figurative language and show how its use can enhance mood, characterization, and theme.

- Students may use this category to focus on a single word and the connotation of it. I've often thought of making word choice its own category—students could consider why the author chose a certain word over another. For now, that idea remains in the Language category in my class, but you may want to try it on its own.

Trace the Title

Directions to Students

You read a passage that seems to directly relate to the title of the entire text. What is it, and how does it relate? Does it mean something deeper? Does it touch upon a theme? Perhaps the title doesn't seem to appear in the book at all—so what could it mean? Why did the author choose these words as the title?

Category Description

"I want to write about the title of the whole book. I just got what it meant!" Rachel said in one of my classes. "Can we write about the title? Mine's a good one," Luke said in another. Students know they can create categories as needed, but the student requests for this one became so prevalent that I added it to our official list.

One reason students like to write about titles is because it simply feels so gratifying to read a passage and suddenly "get" the title of the whole book. It feels like you've arrived! It feels like the key that unlocks the deepest meaning of the work. And in most cases, that's exactly true—titles frequently indicate themes (think of *The Outsiders* or *To Kill a Mockingbird*). And even if titles simply refer to main characters (*The Giver*; *The Book Thief*; *The Great Gatsby*) or settings (*The House on Mango Street*; *Wuthering Heights*) or plots (*The Curious Incident of the Dog in the Night-Time*; *Looking for Alaska*), they warrant explanation. Very often, titles refer to a seemingly minor but incredibly significant line in the text (*Their Eyes Were Watching God*; *Me Talk Pretty One Day*) that subtly captures the theme. And sometimes, titles allude to other famous works (*The Sound and the Fury*; *Things Fall Apart*; *The Fault in Our Stars*), and students delight in discovering the source and applying it to the text.

Encouraging students to examine titles of works pushes them to consider not only the elements previously mentioned, but also the question of author's craft. A colleague of mine, Cyndi Roe, requires her students to *always* title their own work, no matter how brief or seemingly insignificant, because she believes it shows the writer has control over the material. Effective titles tie an entire text together; having students question titles will make them question the heart of the text and will deepen their thinking about the work as a whole.

Student Examples

Trace the Title for *Everything, Everything* (Nicola Yoon) by Blanca, Grade 10

The title of the book is *Everything, Everything*. When I started reading it I continued wondering why that was its title. Throughout the book the narrator says "Everything" at the end of many sentences but I still didn't understand what was its meaning. At the end of the book, Maddy gives us a review about her favorite book, *The Little Prince*, and she says, "Spoiler alert: Love is worth everything. Everything" (pg. 302). That's when I understood that she is talking about love. It made sense in that moment because everything she does since she meets Olly is for love, for him and for the world. She put her life at risk for Olly and to get to know the world and actually start living. Sometimes we do things for love and we don't know if they are right or wrong but it is worth taking risks.

> **O** Blanca pinpoints the exact line containing the title—not necessarily an easy task—and she recognizes the significance.

> **O** Blanca expands the book's theme to life in general.

Trace the Title for *Everything, Everything* (Nicola Yoon) by Sarah, Grade 10

The title of the novel *Everything, Everything* is very fitting to the story and encases the two sides of the main character, Maddy. Maddy has a sickness in which she cannot leave her house because she is allergic to the outside. On the front of the book, the first "Everything" is bland and only had a small paper airplane next to it. The "Everything" under it has many wild colors and various things in the world. The way I interpreted this, the two Everythings are the two different lives she had in the book. The bland Everything is the life she has inside her house where she cannot see anyone or experience things in the world. The more elaborate Everything represents everything Maddy was missing before she decided to leave her house, which is also everything she experienced in Hawaii. In the story, Maddy says, "I was happy before I met [Olly]. But I'm alive now, and those are not the same thing" (Yoon 181). There was so much Maddy felt she was missing while trapped in her house; once she got a chance to leave her house and experience the world, she felt her life had a whole new meaning.

> **N** *Happy* versus *alive* is an unusual opposition. How are they different?

> **O** Sarah is writing about the same book as Blanca, but uses the cover art as part of her evidence! The discussion between these two students would be wonderful.

Teaching Notes

- Encourage students to Google a title if they've reached the end of a book and do not see where the title came from. Perhaps the title contains unknown words or connotations, and a simple search can help them tie the title to the text.

- Often, students don't realize when they're missing allusions—how can they? Again, a quick search could solve it, or at least introduce the connection. That's what Maggie (grade 10) found when she researched "Tender Is the Night" and discovered that Fitzgerald was referring to Keats' poem "Ode to a Nightingale." She was able to make some connections between Fitzgerald's Abe and the narrator of "Nightingale." Although her thoughts required more study of the poem, her efforts at researching the allusion led to a more sophisticated understanding of the novel.

- If a student's RR seems too obvious, don't be afraid to ask follow-up questions. For example, if a student wrote, "The title is *The Giver* because it is about the old man who gives memories," and somehow does not go any deeper with the remaining four sentences, you might ask: "Is the Giver the only main character? Why wasn't the book named *Jonah*? Who is more important, the Giver or Jonah? Why? Could there be more than one Giver in the book?" Use specific questions to get the student thinking.

- Make sure students understand that not all titles have just one meaning. Sometimes a title is purposefully crafted to suggest several meanings at once. *The Outsiders* is a good example of a title like this. The "outsiders" could refer to the Greasers, of course, but with a little probing, students should be able to see how even Cherry, Bob, and Randy, and each of the Greasers individually were outsiders in their own way. Have students think of other titles of books and movies that suggest different meanings and encourage them to explore different possibilities when they use the Trace the Title category.

9

Categories for Examining Structure

The Joy of Genre

Directions to Students

Specifically identify the genre of the text you're reading. How does knowing the genre influence your reading? Find a quote and explain how knowing the genre helps you understand it.

Category Description

If you've read the student samples closely so far, you might have noticed that students tend to call everything a *novel*. When pushed, they might use more specific labels such as *poetry* or *nonfiction*, but they struggle with anything more—even accessing the word *drama* can be a challenge.

Identifying genre is important for several reasons. First, genre is always connected to purpose. An author may want to express something deep and meaningful about the environment, but whether he does that in a poem or an op-ed, an informational article or a dystopian novel, depends on his intentions. Being clear about genre helps readers consider the purpose behind what they're reading.

Readers also have certain expectations of genre that frame their responses in important ways. When readers know a novel is fantasy, for example, they accept all sorts of anomalies (in setting, detail, plot) that would cause confusion in realistic fiction. If they're reading historical fiction, readers expect the basic details of history to be accurate. Or think about how critical it is to understand the difference between news and opinion in the morning paper. They may look similar, but they fulfill very different intentions. Differences in genre may be nuanced, but they *should* matter to readers.

When identifying genre, I encourage students to use precise and established terms, such as *autobiography* or *aphorism* or *sonnet*, if they can. However, if they don't know the official term, I ask them to explain the genre as specifically as possible in their own words. Students might say something like, "It's a story, but it's also advice for living," or "It's a poem that is part of a longer made-up story." These descriptions show me that students are really trying to apply whatever prior knowledge they have about genre. In individual conferences, I can help them learn the necessary academic language.

Student Examples

The Joy of Genre for
The Handmaid's Tale (Margaret Atwood)
by Shannon, Grade 10

The Handmaid's Tale is a science fiction story set in a dystopian society known as Gilead, in which the totalitarian regime controls everything. Women are prohibited from voting, reading, and writing, and have had other freedoms removed. The narrator was starved of these most basic freedoms so much so that the simple act of holding a pen brought her sheer joy: "The pen between my fingers is sensuous, alive almost, I can feel its power, the power of the words it contains . . ." (Atwood 186). This novel was written to express an example of society if all of the rights that women had gained were reversed. A futuristic, dystopian society is an excellent—and perhaps the only—option to successfully execute such a literary work and make it seem almost believable. The genre of science fiction perfectly fits the novel's setting of a dystopian society set in the future.

N Is this world really so far-fetched? Can you think of other historical books, or examples in history, where these events actually happened in some way?

O Shannon highlights an important tenet of science fiction.

The Joy of Genre for
A Dog's Purpose (W. Bruce Cameron)
by Noah, Grade 10

N How do the two novels differ, fantasy-wise? What is the overall purpose of fantasy? Why do we like reading and seeing it?

The genre of *A Dog's Purpose* is fantasy. However, the story fits but doesn't fit all at the same time. "As I sat in the sun on the wooden dock that jutted out into the pond, I knew this to be true: my name was Buddy, and I was a good dog" (pg. 1). This beginning sentence explains why it falls under fantasy. It is from the perspective of a dog so therefore it is fantasy, right? Well throughout the rest of the book it addresses many real life issues and shows what human lives are like in the perspective of dogs. Everything but the perspective is not fantasy at all and rather more of a realistic fiction. It really isn't a fantasy novel in the sense of a *Lord of the Rings* but rather its own kind of genre.

O Noah narrows the genre down to fantasy, and then subdivides fantasy into a continuum of sorts. He is thinking deeply here about genre.

Teaching Notes

- Resist telling students the genres of texts before you read them. Instead, say, *Here's a text I want you to read. First of all, what genre is it, do you think?* Let students judge based on the form, title, and any other information they can glean from a first glance. After reading, you can talk more about the genre, using content as criteria as well. Through this practice, the question *What genre is this?* will hopefully become a habit of mind.

- Students often point out how the purposes of genres overlap and enhance each other in a single text. For example, Cam (grade 10) wrote that although *Tuesdays with Morrie* is a "nonfiction narrative," it also "serves as a self-help book." Jules (grade 7) noted that even though *Eye of Minds* "is in the science fiction genre," the author "plays to romance readers by foreshadowing a relationship beyond friendship between the main character and his best friend." And Carlee (grade 10) appreciated that "The River-Merchant's Wife" was "a letter and a poem at the same time," with an intended recipient. Encourage students to think about how some texts seem to fulfill the purposes of several genres at once.

Note the Narrator

Directions to Students

In fiction, you realize something important about the author's choice of narrator. What is it? Why do you think the author chose this particular narrator's point of view? How might the text be different with a different narrator?

Category Description

This category addresses the question of point of view—a crucial decision by an author telling a story. Perhaps the narrator is a major or minor character in the first person; perhaps it is an all-knowing, outside voice in the third person. A first-person narrator automatically has a limited perspective and as a character will be colored by his own motivations, feelings, and personality. Thus, all first-person narrators are, to some degree, unreliable—but *how* unreliable is the question. A third-person omniscient narrator is considered highly reliable, and a third-person limited narrator can only reveal so much. Some students will even choose books that have a second-person narrator, which draws the reader right into the story. The choice of narrator determines the flow and angle of the plot; it can create suspense, dramatic irony, or mood. I want students not only to notice the narration but also to ask themselves why the author chose it as the best vehicle for the tale.

As with other RRs, this category asks students to take a giant idea—point of view—and tie it down to a single sentence in their explanation. In some first-person texts, this will be easy: perhaps there is a sentence in which the narrator identifies himself or reveals his motivations clearly. But in other texts, this will prove difficult. Students may have to choose seemingly insignificant passages and imagine alternative narrators to formulate a response. Either way, they will practice the habit of finding textual evidence for even their broadest thoughts.

Student Samples

Note the Narrator for *A Separate Peace* (John Knowles)
by Olivia, Grade 10

N How do you know Finny *wasn't* jealous? Are there other examples of Gene's unreliability? Do you think the author planted clues in Gene's narration on purpose?

One thing that's very curious about the story is the fact that we are getting all of the events and descriptions through Gene's perspective. It makes me wonder how the story would be different were it told from a different narrator. The reader must keep in mind that we are seeing characters through Gene's eyes. After slight inspection, it is clear that he tends to spin things in his mind, which don't always turn out right in the real world. For example, Gene convinces himself that as he is jealous of Finny's athletic and personal abilities, Finny is jealous of his academic ones. He says, "We were even after all, even in enmity. The deadly rivalry was on both sides after all" (PDF). Here it becomes clear that the reader should start bringing Gene's narration into question.

O Olivia is questioning Gene's reliability as a narrator.

N Why do you think the author choose Gene as the narrator?

Note the Narrator for *It's Kind of a Funny Story* (Ned Vizzini)
by Becca, Grade 10

The narrator, Craig, is placed in a psychiatric ward due to his extreme depression and anxiety, which were causing him to have severe suicidal thoughts. His fears and worries about everyday were [about] miniscule [things]. However, Craig's perspective on life completely changed the way he perceived situations, events, his own actions, and others' actions, in a negative way. This can be seen throughout the novel as Craig explains his troubles and challenges in a pessimistic, doubtful and defeated sort of manner. "I lie there thinking about everything I've done is a failure, death and failure, and there's no hope for me except being homeless, because I'm never going to be able to hold a job, because everyone else is so much smarter" (Vizzini 119). There are many instances similar to this throughout the book where Craig sets the mood for the entire story. Personally, I thought the technique of using Craig as the narrator was helpful, so the audience could grasp the concepts and feel the same emotions he was feeling.

N Are there any drawbacks to having Craig as the narrator? What do you think the author weighed in his mind when choosing a narrator for this book?

O Becca ties point of view to mood.

Teaching Notes

- Aside from the traditional minilessons about first-person, third-person, limited, and omniscient narration, a fun minilesson would be to discuss the difference between reliable and unreliable narrators and to brainstorm examples. Start with a story the students have read, such as Poe's "The Tell-Tale Heart," and ask questions such as: *Did you trust that this narrator was telling the truth? Did you ever feel like the narrator was leaving out important information? When did you realize the narrator was lying or crazy?* Then ask students what an author can gain with an unreliable narrator.

- To show students how point of view changes how a story is told, you might give them a basic, silly plot and have them retell it with different narrators. For example, a plot like this: *On a city corner at rush hour, a man is selling hot dogs. Across the street, a boy is walking his dog. The dog smells the hot dogs and runs across the street causing a middle-aged businessman to slam on his breaks and a ninety-year-old woman to rear-end him. As the dog reaches the cart and hot dogs fly everywhere, a baby in a stroller claps.* In pairs, students can retell the story as the dog, the boy, the vendor, the man, the woman, the baby, or as a third-person narrator. After, discuss the advantages, disadvantages, and reliability of each voice.

- Point out that often an author has to research a voice for it to be convincing. Brainstorm examples of character narrators that might have required research. Start with any adult author who has written a novel from the perspective of an adolescent (as John Green does). What would this adult have to research to understand contemporary adolescent life?

- Students will gravitate to this category when reading books with strong first-person narrators. But encourage them to question third-person choices as well. For example, Modupe (grade 10) noted that "because [*The Fever Code*] is an action novel," the third-person narration "really helps show perspective." There are advantages to telling a story in third-person omniscient narration, because the author does not have to narrow information based on a single character's knowledge. Be sure students learn to recognize and appreciate this as well.

Connect Form and Content

Directions to Students

What about the form or structure (the way lines, sentences, paragraphs, even whole chapters look on the page) influences the content and meaning? Explain.

Category Description

This category overlaps some with both The Joy of Genre and Seeing the Sentences. But as a lover of literature, I cannot emphasize enough to students how form shapes and creates meaning. Contemporary young adult literature especially capitalizes on this, often dropping texts, emails, charts, sketches, poetry, and letters right into traditional paragraphed narration. With this category, I want students to consider what happens in their thinking when they become very aware of the form and structure of the writing as they're reading. And of course *most* of the nonfiction that readers encounter in both print and digital media uses form in all kinds of interesting ways to shape content and meaning. There's a big difference between reporting data in a paragraph and reporting it in an infographic, and critical readers know that form can trans*form* content in important ways.

This category, Connect Form and Content, actually existed first on my list of RR possibilities; later, I wanted students to have more of a zoom lens (Seeing the Sentences) as well as a wide-angle lens (The Joy of Genre) to think about as well. These categories require a sophisticated eye, and many students have to stretch to respond to them, but with practice, they refine their skills, gain confidence, and begin to see more complex connections between form and content.

Student Examples

Connect Form and Content for *Girl in Pieces* (Kathleen Glasgow) by Maddie, Grade 10

> **N** Why did the author do this? Is it more effective than if all the chapters were the same length?

In this book, I've noticed that the chapter length has a deeper meaning. Most chapters are typically 3–5 pages and contain dialogue and stories. However, every once in a while there will be a chapter that is shorter than ½ of a page. It's within these chapters that you can get a true understanding of Charlie's emotions. The sentences are either short and to the point or long with metaphors. I see this as a reflection of what Charlie's emotions are. When she gets into a really sad, depressive state, these chapters come about. When she's doing okay, the chapters go back to their normal length. For instance, when Charlie realizes that she is heading back down the same path as before by entering a relationship with Riley, the chapter is very short. She says things like "All of it is wrong. I see it. I understand it" and "It's too late, anyway, you see: I've already fallen in" (Glasgow 252). Her words are very short but when you piece together the chapter you can see that she realizes that it was a mistake but there is nothing she can do about it now.

> **O** Maddie recognizes that the author is using chapter length to communicate the character's feelings.

Connect Form and Content for *Simon vs. The Homo Sapiens Agenda* (Becky Albertalli) by Sophie, Grade 10

> **O** Sophie really pinpoints a human trait here—the desire to look into someone's personal correspondence, even though our cultural values prohibit it!

Throughout the book, Simon emails his close friend and future boyfriend, Blue. "Eventually I worked up the courage . . . then I wrote my email address. My secret Gmail account" (PDF). However, instead of simply saying that they emailed each other, or summarizing the emails, the book showed the emails. They were more or less in email format, which really added to the connectedness of the story altogether. Instead of feeling like somebody is retelling a story, it feels like the reader is truly spectating the events. While it's not a good thing to read someone's emails in real life without permission, people are still curious, so it's really interesting to have been able to read what Simon and Blue have chatted about throughout the book. This format definitely added a lot to the story, since a lot of the plot focused on their little emailing escapades, and I believe it was a clever choice to add the emails into the book in this format.

> **N** What other modern-day technological realities do you think authors have to make choices about when they write?

Teaching Notes

- Point out choices or changes in form whenever possible. If the class is reading a common text, ask questions such as *What do you notice about this chapter length? How does the look of the text on the page change, and why? Does this section look different than the others, and why?*

- Students may even notice a format given to certain characters. Hannah (grade 10) found it appropriate that Morrie from *Tuesdays with Morrie* often spoke in aphorisms, because he so clearly imparted wisdom. Cameron (grade 10) noticed that when Krishna spoke his most meaningful lines in "The Yoga of Knowledge," the form within the story changed from drama to poetry. Encourage students to always question changes in form.

Interesting Intro

Directions to Students

You think the author's introduction is interesting, clever, or engaging. Tell what the author did to make it so interesting, and why you think that is effective.

Category Description

Students are trained early on, often formulaically, to write engaging introductions to five-paragraph essays. When I first added this category to my list, I wanted students to notice the techniques professional authors used in shorter, nonfiction pieces, such as op-eds and personal essays, to help them in their own essay writing. However, students soon started to use this category for other genres such as longer fiction and poetry. This makes perfect sense. Introductions, or beginnings of any kind, are painstakingly shaped to draw readers in and to set the mood, tone, style, and in fiction, plot; I want students to be aware not only of the craft, but also of the groundwork of information woven into those first few words. How well the student understands the introduction can affect her engagement with the rest of the text. I want students to have the space to practice noticing introductions. With patience, they will become more adept at decoding them.

Student Examples

Interesting Intro for *The Eye of Minds* (James Dashner) by Mark, Grade 7

The author just surprises the reader by opening with a suicidal girl. "Tanya had just climbed over the railing of the Golden Gate Bridge, cars zooming by on the road, and was leaning back towards the open air" (pg. 1). Suicide is controversial and the author opens his book that way. It appeals to me because most people are timid to joke about something like ending your life: "I know it's water down there but it might as well be concrete. You'll be flat as a pancake the second you hit" (pg. 1). The author's technique of surprising the reader is captivating.

> O Mark notices that the author uses the techniques of surprise and even a taboo topic.

> N Did this make you want to keep reading? What specifically did you want to find out?

> N Who said this to Tanya? What are some character traits for this person that you learn right on the first page?

Interesting Intro for "The Story of Daedalus and Icarus" by Aidan, Grade 10

The intro to this story is *in medias res.* This means it drops you right into the action of the story. This story starts off with the conflict and it low-key drops hints of the setting and why they're where they are. It says, "Homesick for his homeland, Daedalus hated Crete and his long exile there, but the sea held him . . . 'surely the sky is open, and that's the way we'll go'" (Lines 1–2, 4–5). *In medias res* kept the story interesting and kept my attention from beginning to end.

> N Explain to me exactly where these are in your quote.

> N Why do you think this technique is so captivating? Can you think of other stories or movies that begin *in medias res?*

Teaching Notes

- As you encounter them in shared texts, point out different introductory techniques. Ovid's technique, *in medias res*, is a traditional one; other techniques such as using vivid sensory detail, a personal anecdote, or a question can also be effective. But students will also notice things for themselves and put their ideas in their own words. Mark's RR doesn't mention *in medias res* but describes it in different terms. Olivia, grade 7, wrote an RR about the prologue in *Me Before You*; a prologue is not something I would have thought to include in a lesson on introductions before reading the RR.

- Of course, having students write engaging introductions to their own essays and stories will help them notice the introductions in published works. Encourage students to try the techniques they've noticed in their reading when they write.

- A fun challenge could be to ask students where an introduction *ends* in a piece. Ask students: *Why do you think the introduction ends here? What is finished? What new step is beginning?* By delineating an end, students can also try to define what elements an introduction includes.

Clever Conclusion

Directions to Students

You think the author's conclusion or clincher is really effective. Tell what technique the author used and why it works.

Category Description

Like the Interesting Intro category, I created this category to draw students' attention to conclusions in short, nonfiction pieces, but students began applying the category to other texts as well. Conclusions are the doors out of a piece, and authors want to make the passage meaningful and memorable.

For readers, this means noticing not only how the plot ends or the content wraps up; it means leaving a piece with a sense of its deeper meaning and connection to life—ideally. In reality, students often are confounded with conclusions. Some expect all questions to be answered, but instead, the author creates additional questions. Some expect a clear summary of the theme, but the author leaves only an important symbol. Some expect more action, and turn the page to find nothing else. Whatever their expectations going in to a conclusion, students should practice seeing what's actually there and considering what the author's purpose might be in concluding this way.

Student Examples

Clever Conclusion for *The Young Elites* (Marie Lu)
by Isabel, Grade 7

On page 344, paragraph 2, the author wraps up this invigorating novel with a well-written sentence: "But tonight, we stay where we are, holding on, lost in the dark." Not only do I think this sentence suggests closure between Adelina and Violetta after the wild events of the book, but it also hints to a sequel. With the "but" in the beginning of the sentence, I believe action is suggested for a sequel. But this particular work of literature ends with two unique sisters, locked in an embrace. The solution to the brief conflict between the sisters is what really gives the ending a sense of satisfaction when you close the cover.

> **N** Did you see this coming at all? How?

> **O** Excellent close reading here.

> **N** What do you think it will be about?

Clever Conclusion for *Flipped* (Wendelin Van Draanen)
by Olivia, Grade 7

The author concludes the book with Bryce planting Juli a sycamore tree in her yard while she watches and thinks about him. This part refers to an earlier event, when Juli's favorite sycamore tree got cut down. It changes her views on Bryce and makes her want to know him better. "Maybe there is more to Bryce Loski than I know. Maybe it's time to meet him in the proper light" (pg. 212). It gives a strong, happy ending to the book.

> **N** Is the sycamore tree a symbol in the novel?

> **N** What does this mean?

Teaching Notes

- If students are disappointed with a conclusion, remind them that all writing is a series of choices by the author. Nudge students to move from an idea like "This ending stinks!" to questions such as "What is the author trying to say with this ending?"

- At the same time, help students pinpoint why they didn't like the ending. Ask questions such as *What do you feel is missing? What parts seem unclear or unrelated to the rest of the text?*

- Similarly, encourage students to pinpoint exactly what they may *like* about a conclusion. Ask questions such as: *What theme is emphasized here? What is the final imagery, and what does it mean? What specific problem is solved? What is the mood or final feeling of the text, and why? What is the reader left to think about once the text has ended?*

10

Categories for Making Advanced Connections

Crossover

Directions to Students

Tie together two aspects of a text. For example, explain how the setting affects the mood, how the conflict relates to the theme, how a certain character trait led to a conflict, how a symbol reveals a theme, or how the setting is important for the plot. Identify and link together any two literary elements. Label your two elements at the top of your RR.

Category Description

In other RR categories, students might investigate setting, characterization, symbol, or theme on their own; but for this category, I want students to go beyond examination of a single element in a text and begin to see how multiple elements fit together. Students will often mention more than one literary element in other RRs—they naturally frame their thoughts as "crossovers" quite frequently. However, by making crossover its own category, I want students to realize they are doing it so they can be more intentional in their thinking.

What makes this category a bit challenging is that although some suggestions for connections are given in the directions, students must make their own connections from scratch. I am always pleasantly surprised to see students choose this category when they could have chosen something more straightforward. They do it because they enjoy the challenge.

Student Examples

> ### Crossover: Theme from Conflict, for *Tuesdays with Morrie* (Mitch Albom), by Danny, Grade 10
>
> In *Tuesdays with Morrie*, the theme was about what one can learn about life through death. I labeled this a crossover because the theme is directly derived from the conflict. Morrie is told that he only has a short period left to live and instead of living the rest of his life depressed, he decides to make the best of it, which gives us the theme. "The truth is, once you learn how to die, you learn how to live" (PDF.) This quote shows Morrie's attitude about the news of his shortened life and how he is planning on living out the rest of his years. This gives us our theme through our conflict.

N What exactly is Morrie's attitude here? What words would you use to describe it?

> ### Crossover: Mood Affecting Setting, for "The River-Merchant's Wife" (Li Po), by Camille, Grade 10
>
> In this letter written by the River-Merchant's wife, she is in a very depressed mode. But in the beginning she is a young pure girl. "I played about the front gate, pulling flowers" (286). She seems to be very innocent on her own, as I can tell from the setting of the flowers which can be a symbol of happiness. Then later on when her husband is out at his job and has been gone for awhile, her mood seems to change. This is affecting the setting: "By the gate now, the moss is grown . . . too deep to clear them away" (287). She is now all alone and misses her husband very much, as the moss can symbolize how much she does miss him and is sad without him.

N What, exactly, is the mood here?

O Camille reversed the setting/mood equation: Teachers often tell students to look for moods that are created by settings, but Camille posits that the setting changes based on the speaker's mood.

N Do you see any other examples of the setting affecting the mood in this poem?

Teaching Notes

- Model making these connections for students as often as possible. Character traits create conflicts that eventually lead to themes; settings and figurative language create moods; sensory details and dialogue create characters. Well-written texts fit together in a myriad of ways.

- As an introductory lesson, it might help to create a chart with several rows such as this:

Charting Connections Inside a Text

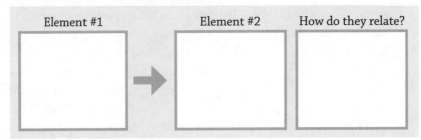

Students could work together on the chart above using a common text, thinking of ways one element impacts another. This will help them in writing not only crossovers but other RRs as well, because they will learn to ask themselves, "Does this element relate to anything else?"

Archetype Alert

Directions to Students

Identify an archetype in the text and tell what it means, why it's an archetype, and where else you've seen it in literature. Then ask: "Why would the author choose to use it here?"

Category Description

Understanding the concept of archetypes can be difficult at first; my sophomores have usually not heard the term before. But once they grasp the meaning, they start to see archetypes everywhere. How could they not? Archetypes are the building blocks of the psyche. As humans, we know about archetypes whether we realize we do or not.

Basic character archetypes include the hero, the villain, and the wise, old advisor. The hero's journey is an archetypal plot. Students can identify these easily by middle school. But when students start to pick up on archetypal symbols, such as doves or serpents, or archetypal settings, such as a great flood or dark forest, things get interesting. By making archetypes its own category, I want to draw attention to their prevalence in literature and put students on the lookout.

Student Examples

Archetype Alert for
The Epic of Gilgamesh
by Robby, Grade 10

Gilgamesh's encounter with Utnapishtim is very important. It's an archetype in many stories—going to a wise, old man for advice and wisdom is very common. He said to Gilgamesh, "But man's life is short, at any moment it can be snapped . . ." This advice is motivational and deep. Gilgamesh will use it wisely most likely and help him conquer his fear of death (pg. 178).

N Can you think of other examples of the wise, old advisor?

O Robby could have chosen an easier archetype such as the hero or hero's journey, but he found a more subtle one in the wise advisor.

N How could this advice help conquer a fear of death? Explain.

Archetype Alert for *The Thousand and One Nights*
by Destiny, Grade 10

Within "The Tale of King Sindbad and the Falcon," it states on page 93, "The king raised his eyes and saw in the tree an enormous serpent spitting its venom down the trunk." The king noticed too late, and had already cut the wings off of the falcon. This was the falcon who had saved his life. It is a common theme throughout all literature that a serpent brings only bad luck. For instance, within the Bible, there is also an evil serpent. This serpent convinces Adam and Eve to eat from the tree of knowledge, although it was not allowed. In addition, a serpent starts the final battle within the stories of King Arthur. This creature frightens a man, making him raise his sword. Those who were battling them saw this as a threat and the battle began. I believe that the authors chose to use serpents as a sign of evil and to show the innocence in their actions. In each story, it could be blamed on the serpent rather than the person.

> N Can you add any contemporary examples of the archetypal evil serpent?

> N Are all the people in your examples completely blameless?

Teaching Notes

- Point out archetypes during reading whenever possible. It's as simple as asking something like, *Can you think of any other stories in which the main character is forbidden to be with her love? Could this be an archetype?*

- To introduce archetypes, I like to use "the dark forest" as a starting point. Students can immediately describe a dark forest as scary, mysterious, bad, or dangerous. When I ask them to think of stories, they name Snow White, Little Red Riding Hood, and Harry Potter.

- Keep a running list of archetypes on a poster somewhere in your room. As archetypes reveal themselves in class readings, add to the list.

What Would _____ Say?

Directions to Students

Fill in with the name of an author, historical figure, scientist, scholar, or teacher. How would that person respond to a certain spot in the text? Why? Be sure to explain the person's philosophy/focus and how it relates to the text.

Category Description

This fun category arose as a result of a student's response, as described in Chapter 2, on p. 16. Even before that, students often connected a reading or theme with something another teacher said in class. These thoughts from other teachers would be related to their content area or were just part of a personal philosophy. Either way, I was delighted by the connections—it meant students were thinking about their learning outside of the classroom and seeing connections among ideas.

I also noticed that students sometimes included information in their essays that came from personal interest or study about a certain individual. They would mention a historical figure in their introduction or conclusion; some even crafted whole theses around a philosopher's theory or a scientist's finding. I realized that some students are budding experts in the fields that interest them—why not let them use their knowledge in English class?

Sometimes, students will use authors or characters we've studied in English class for this category. For example, while reading _Sully_, Matt wrote a What Would Confucius Say RR. Regardless of the person students choose for this category, making outside connections will deepen their understanding of the text.

Student Examples

What Would Mr. Hanyon Say? for Confucius' *The Analects*
by Arla, Grade 10

The fifth aphorism on page 269 reminded me of Mr. Hanyon, our athletic director. He strongly approves of positive reinforcement from captains/team leaders. The aphorism said, "Keep order among them by chastisements, and they will flee from you, and lose all self respect . . . Keep order by ritual and they will keep their self-respect and come to you of their own accord." I think Mr. Hanyon would like this quote because it shows the power of positive leadership. Rather than the leader (in this case of the government) being "bossy" and bringing his/her team down, he/she is leading by example. This leader is showing his/her team/community the right way to act, rather than punishing them for acting improperly.

> **O** Arla is drawing from her experience as both the captain of her sports team and a mentee of Mr. Hanyon.

> **N** What do you think Confucius means by "ritual" in your quote? Do sports teams have rituals that help them remain orderly and positive?

What Would Hammurabi Say? for *The Thousand and One Nights*
by Jakob, Grade 10

When reading the story from *The One Thousand and One Nights*, "The Fisherman and the Jinnee," I was reminded of another historical writing of the Middle East. This writing is Hammurabi's set of two hundred eighty-two laws known as Hammurabi's code. In this code there are many laws, but many of them boil down to the main idea that if someone does wrong to another, the wronged person has the authority to pay the other back with the same wrong. The most famous instance of this would be the example of "an eye for an eye and a tooth for a tooth," meaning that if someone knocks your tooth out, you would have the privilege of knocking their tooth out. When the fisherman says that "if [the jinnee] had been willing to spare [him], Allah would have been merciful . . ." he is saying that the jinnee would be repaid with mercy if he was merciful. However, the jinnee was not merciful, and in return to his mercilessness, he received no mercy from the fisherman. I think the Hammurabi would say that the fisherman is right to be merciless to the jinnee because the fisherman is following one of his codes.

> **O** Jakob is drawing from his own prior knowledge here.

> **N** Do you think this cultural value exists today? How?

Teaching Notes

- Be sure students explain not only their text example but also the outside person invoked for this category, as Jakob did. If a student merely writes, "Einstein would agree" or "Eleanor Roosevelt wouldn't like this," push him to explain why.

- When students write about other teachers, try to photograph or copy the RR and drop it in your colleague's mailbox. It really makes them happy to know that students not only were listening, but also were able to apply what they were taught!

Crazy RR Challenge

Directions to Students

Go to the website http://literary-devices.com/. Look at the "Quick List" of literary devices on the left. *Pick one you don't know*, read the definition and example, and see if you can find it in the reading. Explain the term, where it is in the reading, and its effect.

Category Description

I'm always pleasantly surprised when students choose this category. I wrote it as an over-the-top challenge for anyone who felt a little tired of the regular categories and needed to reengage. I didn't know if students would actually make the effort to teach themselves a new term and then try to write about it—why spend time learning something like chiasmus or synecdoche when you can write something about character or setting? But I underestimated my students! Many try this site because they're curious or because they want a challenge—and of course, an RR is a safe place to try something new.

I like this site, literarydevices.com, in particular because it lists over eighty-five terms and gives a definition and example for each, with a clean layout and minimal advertisements (at the time of this printing there is only one at the very top). When students go to the site, I suspect they click on several terms before finding one they feel that they can use. And although many of the terms are advanced, the site includes more basic concepts such as alliteration, mood, onomatopoeia, and puns. I tell the students to not be intimidated; rather, they should feel accomplished with all the terms they *do* recognize and not be afraid to add one more to their repertoire.

Student Examples

Crazy RR Challenge for "Form, Shadow, Spirit" (T'ao Ch'ien) by Cameron, Grade 10

> **N** How would the title feel different with the word *and* in it?

The title of this poem, I found out, is called an asyndeton. An asyndeton is when an author or writer purposely leaves out conjunctions when writing. The title of this poem being, "Form, Shadow, Spirit" (pg. 282) is exactly that. This literary device is used to emphasize that each word in the title is significant on its own and doesn't need one another to be important to the poem. Each section in the poem is a separation of form, shadow, spirit and the asyndeton is used to show that in the title. An asyndeton is somewhat rare as a literary device and used in more of an ancient literature sense.

> **N** Are you sure about this? Try a quick search and see what comes up.

Crazy RR Challenge for *Brisingr* (Christopher Paolini) by Katya, Grade 10

Kennings is a compound, hyphenated phrase used to refer to a person, place, or thing. It is traditionally used in old English, Germanic, or Norse works, but I found a close match in the "speech" of the dragon Saphira. The chapter "Message in a Mirror" is from Saphira's point of view, and she tends to name objects using a compound description. She calls

Eragon's tent a "cloth-shell," which makes sense because it is a hollow structure made of canvas (Paolini 530). Then, later, she thinks of a magical mirage of Eragon as a "water-shadow-ghost" (Paolini 530). She does not think of clothing in terms of shirts, pants, and boots, but rather "plant-cloth-hides" that swish and "skin-paw-coverings" that "[thud] against the ground" (Paolini 531). What's interesting is that she only uses these phrases within her own mind; when conversing with others, she uses nouns and adjectives just like a human would. Paolini writes kennings into Saphira's thoughts to differentiate her, even in the mind, from the humans and humanoid beings in the story.

O Not only does Katya identify the use of kennings, she notices that it creates the character.

N Why does the character do this? Is she hiding her dragonness or trying to fit in?

Teaching Notes

- You will find that students often misuse the new terms. This is understandable, because they are teaching themselves a difficult idea and trying to apply it. For example, Clay (grade 10) wrote about the term *euphemism* in an RR. He defined it correctly but was a bit off on the interpretation. Treat these opportunities as teachable moments.

- When you discover that someone has written a crazy RR challenge, use it as a minilesson for the whole class. Write the term on the board and have a brief discussion about its meaning and the student's application of it. Applaud the student's willingness to take a risk in new territory.

11

Categories for Applying Literary Theories

To develop the questions students explore in each of these categories, I used information online from the Purdue Online Writing Lab (Brizee et al. 2015)—a site with a wealth of helpful writing resources and instructional materials.

New Historicist Criticism

Directions to Students

The New Historicists believe a text is inextricably intertwined with the time and culture of its author. This means that the author's era and culture shape the text. Ask yourself:

- How does the text demonstrate the culture of the author?
- What specific elements, such as language, characters, or events, show the culture and time period of the author?
- Does the text seem to support or criticize the people and events in the author's time period?

Category Description

Admittedly, this category can be difficult—I'm asking students to identify the author's era and culture, and to apply that knowledge to the author's work. Because I teach world literature, opportunities abound: An idea as simple as Homer's culture believing in the Greek gods and then the appearance of those gods in the *Iliad* would certainly count. What surprises me is when students apply New Historicism criticism to the more modern books they choose for their book club reading. "Even before I looked up the publication date [for *Tuesdays with Morrie*], I could tell that this book was oriented around modern culture because of its focus on money and conformity," Cam wrote in his RR. This is exactly what New Historicists ask readers to do—to wonder, when was this written? How could that have affected the text?

I am delighted with any attempt students make to see the underlying culture and time period of a text. To take a step back from a text and try to put it in context is a sophisticated, intellectual effort; at the same time, it is essential for any serious reader. When students start to understand that texts are tied to authors who are tied to eras, I know they are maturing as thinkers.

Student Examples

New Historicism Criticism for the *Inferno* (Dante) by Chris, Grade 10

N If someone wrote a book like this today, do you think people would understand the author's purpose?

While reading the *Inferno*, I noticed that Dante placed many of his real life enemies in the pits of hell. "They were all shouting: 'At Filippo Argenti!' (Canto 8). This intrigued me as to what Dante meant to accomplish with his work. I began to wonder if Dante wanted to use his poems to discredit his political opponents and personal enemies. Dante was moderately involved in Florentine politics, and he called out perpetrators of simony and corruption through the *Inferno*. I am curious as to whether or not people who lived in Florence in the 1300s were aware of Dante's ulterior motives. To Dante, betrayal and treachery are the highest order of sin. Dante was trying to spread his political and religious ideals through the Divine Comedy.

N Tell me more about the context of this quote. How did you learn this character was an enemy of Dante?

New Historicism Criticism for
Gone with the Wind (Margaret Mitchell)
by Dimitri, Grade 10

When I began reading *Gone with the Wind*, I was hoping that it was a satire. However, I was surprised to learn that Margaret Mitchell is actually from Georgia, and that her portrayal of the war could be taken quite literally. Her writing gives the perspective of southerners during the Civil War, portraying slavery as a fact of life. In fact, as I mentioned in another reading response, the main character, Scarlett, isn't at all bothered by this, nor are any of the other characters. One even calls one of their slaves "[a] smart . . . old darky" (Mitchell 144). Anyone today could say that is not polite in the slightest, yet, the historical perspective makes it seem as though it's perfectly acceptable.

> **N** Is there any indication in the text about how Mitchell herself felt about this?

> **O** Dimitri is linking thoughts from other RRs—an ongoing conversation with the text.

Teaching Note

- A good place to start to help students grasp the concept of this category is with interviews of authors they might know. S. E. Hinton, for example, has written about how she got the idea for *The Outsiders* from events in her own life. Sometimes this kind of information exists as a Q and A in the backs of books, and sometimes separate articles or videos exist.

Feminist Criticism

Directions to Students

Feminists focus on the portrayal and oppression of women in a text. Think about:

- How are the relationships between men and women, and how are they portrayed?

- Who has power in male–female relationships, and how is that demonstrated?

- What are females' roles compared with men's?

- What is the structure of evidence of a patriarchy within the text?

Category Description

Because feminism and questions of equality are part of everyday life, most students are aware of this issue and can apply it to texts to some degree. Many students already think and read with a feminist's eye; of all the criticisms, the feminist critique is the one that comes up most often as an opinion RR before students are formally introduced to the theory categories. Often, students make passionate and shocked critiques of older literature depicting arranged marriages, strict female domestic roles, and abuse. But a feminist critique can be applied to modern literature and nonfiction as well. Ultimately, I want all students to detect the more insidious examples of bias still woven into even the most contemporary texts.

At the same time, feminist theory does not require gender bias or female mistreatment to be invoked as a critique. It can be applied to any text to examine the balance of power between males and females, or how men and women relate to each other in the text. As with all the criticisms, feminist theory is merely a lens through which a text can be examined; by teaching students to view texts from several angles, we help them gain deeper understanding.

Student Examples

> ### Feminist Criticism for *The Bell Jar* (Sylvia Plath)
> ### by Alex, Grade 10
>
> Because of the time period that this was written in, I wasn't surprised to see a lot of old fashioned ideology regarding men and women. Mrs. Willard, Esther's ex-boyfriend's mother, says, "What a man wants is a mate and what a woman wants is infinite security," and, "what a man is is an arrow into the future and what a woman is is the place the arrow shoots off from" (Plath 72). This was sort of confusing to me as I was reading, but I interpreted it as Mrs. Willard finding it hard to fathom that a woman could ever be more than her husband's biggest fan. This notion is clearly foreign to Esther, and I think that has a lot to do with the time period. However, Plath definitely challenges this ideology, because Esther's personality doesn't fully conform to the social norm that says her gender determines her worth in comparison to a man's. There are some times where the writing suggests the opposite, but the vast majority of the novel supports power to women and femininity.

O Alex explains her thought process as she read this quote.

N Can you paraphrase a specific event to support this?

O Alex treads into New Historicism criticism here.

Feminist Criticism for the *Iliad* (Homer)
by Andrew, Grade 10

In lines 300–316, Cassandra has a fit over her brother's death. In many stories, we see females having more emotions than men, and yelling out about it—as shown in this text. Things like "His loving wife and noble mother were the first to fling themselves on the wagon rolling on, the first to tear their hair, embrace his head and a waiting throng of people milled around them." If you heard this in the text, no one would think this is a male. The text makes females seem as they are overreacting and this is not true in all situations. It does not show Hector's father's reaction during this scene, or any other males that would be related to him. It is all females and it is all dramatic. No males. All females being upset. Is this [perception] still present in our world? I firmly believe so.

> **N** How so? Can you think of another example?

> **O** Andrew picks up on the archetypal "hysterical woman."

Teaching Note

- When reading passages with students, especially in a whole-class setting, point out moments where a feminist critique would be interesting and appropriate. Ask questions such as, *How are the woman portrayed here? Who ultimately has power right now? In what ways is the female character equal or unequal to her male counterparts?*

Marxist Criticism

Directions to Students

Marxists look at questions surrounding social class. Consider these questions:

- What social classes are the characters in? How do you know?
- Does one social class seem to have power over another? How do characters from different classes act with each other? Do they clash?
- Does the text as a whole seem to reinforce or promote the values of a certain class?

Description of Category

Students acutely understand socioeconomic class differences in life, and applying that understanding to texts usually comes easily to them. Examining the classes of characters and how those class situations affect them will help students piece out the dynamics at play in a story.

A more difficult endeavor is the final question in the directions: Does the entire text advocate the values of a certain class? This is a more sophisticated question that usually cannot be easily answered. Consider *The Great Gatsby*. One may feel sympathy for Gatsby, or even Daisy, but the book certainly does not promote the values of the Long Island elite. Besides, even though Gatsby was one of them, he really was not, because he climbed into the wealthy class from a lower one. Similarly, *The Outsiders* does not wholly advocate the values of the Greasers, although the reader's sympathy is certainly on their side. One of the book's main purposes is to muddy the lines delineating stereotypical class values. All of these considerations serve to bring students deeper into the heart of a text, and even if only questions remain at the end of a discussion, students will have progressed by following this line of thinking.

Student Examples

Marxist Criticism for *Macbeth* (William Shakespeare)
by Noah, Grade 12

In *Macbeth*, Act I Scene iv, Duncan says, "Sons, kinsmen, thanes, and you whose places are the nearest, know we will establish our estate upon our eldest, Malcolm, whom we name hereafter 'The prince of Cumberland.'" This is an absolute outrage. This whole scene is about Duncan praising Macbeth and how great he is. Even after this point Duncan returns to praising Macbeth and talking about how great he is. It's clear to any unbiased observer that Macbeth should be the next king. Evidently, however, he can't be because of the absurd social class structure. Since Macbeth wasn't born into the royal family he can't be the King, despite him clearly being the most qualified for that post. Furthermore, nothing about Malcolm indicates that he should be allowed to be king. Except for the fact that Malcolm is the son of the king. This strict adherence to social classes is the kind of stuff that destroys societies and is why monarchy is a ridiculous form of government.

> N Is it only confined to monarchies? Are democracies based purely on merit?

> N Are there other examples of this class structure? What are they?

Marxist Criticism for
The Handmaid's Tale (Margaret Atwood)
by Maddie, Grade 10

The entire plot of *The Handmaid's Tale* revolves around social-class like factions which describe a person's role in the society. There are Commanders, Econowives, Marthas, Handmaids, The Commander's Wives, and Unwomen. Offred is a handmaid, which definitively leaves her as the child-bearer of the Commanders. In the eyes of the government, she has no real purpose other than the birthing of children. After being summoned by her Commander she thought, "It's forbidden for us to be alone with the Commanders. We are for breeding purposes . . . There is supposed to be nothing entertaining about us" (p. 136). Each class of these people are seen more as their "job," than humans with souls, minds, and personalities. Even more socially binding is the fact that if you cannot perform your given task, you are sent to the colonies to be eliminated.

> **N** Do you think that labeling the classes helps enforce them?

> **N** Do you think this threat is enough to control everyone in the society? Is there evidence in the text of characters rejecting their role?

Teaching Notes

- A good place to introduce Marxist Theory is with *The Outsiders.* The class structures and their consequences are clearly outlined. Ask students, *Which group has power in this story? How? What specific advantages do the Socs have? What specific disadvantages do the Greasers have? What do Greasers have to work for that Socs don't?*

- Most texts deal with social structure in some way. The dystopian or apocalyptic genres so popular now are painstakingly built on social rankings, as Maddie describes. Point this out whenever possible and call your thinking Marxist criticism, so students realize that the examination of classes has a name. Say things such as, "A Marxist theorist would notice that Katniss [*The Hunger Games*] is a member of the oppressed lower class in this story." This may seem obvious, but naming it will help students become more skilled as they unpack texts.

Psychoanalytical Criticism

Directions to Students

Most psychoanalysis stems from Sigmund Freud's work about the unconscious—the mind "below" our conscious mind that impacts all our decisions. Ask yourself:

- Is any character repressing events from the past? Is any character repressing secret drives or desires?

- Is the Oedipus complex at work here? (Son loves mother and hates father.) Or Electra complex? (Daughter loves father.)

- Do you see any other complexes within characters (Cinderella, Icarus, Superiority, or Inferiority)?

- Are there any other psychological factors at work (a fear or fascination with death, for example)?

Category Description

Most students will be somewhat familiar with the questions about emotions in this category because they are prevalent in popular culture—in talk shows, crime dramas, and even children's shows and movies, such as *Inside Out*. As a culture, we encourage children to talk about their feelings and process their emotions; we tell them to live as their "true selves" and not hide what they feel. Whether they do or not, they understand, on some level, the meaning of it all. They will be able to sense when a character is hiding something or suffering from a past trauma.

They will also understand the basic complexes—they have probably dealt with people who have inferiority or superiority complexes, and with a little explanation, they can grasp the Icarus and Cinderella complexes. In my tenth-grade class, we read *Oedipus Rex*, and although students are understandably grossed out, they get the idea. By suggesting a selection of psychological interpretations, this category will help students understand characters more deeply, and might even help them sort out a bit of real life as well.

Student Examples

Psychoanalytic Criticism for
The Siren (Kiera Cass)
by Modupe, Grade 10

Late in the book, a new character came in. Her name was Padma. "'He threw me in,' she confessed staring at her hands . . . 'No dowry. A girl is too expensive'" (p. 96). This is Padma speaking, talking about her father. Padma had been abused by her father throughout her entire life, and had to sit by and watch when her father abused her mother. While her mother didn't exactly abuse her, she did nothing to stop her father when he would abuse her. Throughout the course of the book, Padma couldn't forget her past like most sirens so. She held onto it, and would often cry when remembering it. Padma likely suffers from Post-Traumatic Stress Disorder due to her past.

> **N** Explain more about what's happening here—what was Padma thrown into?

> **O** Modupe names a psychological condition not mentioned in the directions.

Psychoanalytical Criticism for
the *Iliad* (Homer)
by Katya, Grade 10

There is some Stockholm's syndrome going on in the *Iliad*. Stockholm's syndrome is a condition where a captive begins to develop attachments to his/her captor, and there are quite a few captive "prizes" in the story. Achilles and Briseis clearly have something going on because Achilles drew the "sword from its sheath" to kill Agamemnon for taking her from him (1.200). We know that Achilles loves Briseis, but not if she loves him back. To find out, I did a little Google searching, and the Internet says she did enjoy her captivity until Agamemnon took her away. We know that Achilles and Briseis have a strange relationship because Agamemnon views his girl as a slave and prostitute.

> **N** Do you think Achilles really loves Briseis, or does he do this out of pride for one of his "possessions"?

> **O** Katya also names a psychological condition not given in the directions.

> **N** This thought feels unfinished; can you explain more to me?

Teaching Notes

- You may be surprised where students go when they start thinking through a psychoanalytical lens. In my class, Eryn wrote about Jeanette's "pyromaniac tendencies" as a way of dealing with childhood trauma in *The Glass Castle*; Noah wrote about CJ's bulimia in *A Dog's Purpose*; Emma wrote about Achilles' progression through the stages of grief after Patroclus died; Ryelee wrote about how Gladwell's ideas in *Blink* are supported by Freud's theory on the unconscious. Students know more than we realize about psychology—encourage all efforts they make to name and apply psychological terms and conditions.

- At the same time, clarify their mistakes and incomplete ideas. They are exposed to so many psychological conditions through media, entertainment, and real life, but they will surely have gaps in their understanding. Helping students refine their thinking in this area will go a long way for them outside the classroom.

Gender Studies and Queer Theory

Directions to Students

This lens is influenced by feminist criticism, but seeks to go even further. It is concerned with how gender and sexuality are portrayed in a text. Questions include:

- What aspects of the text seem traditionally masculine, and what aspects seem traditionally feminine? How do the characters fit into these traditional roles?

- Are there aspects or characters that question the masculine/feminine binary? What happens to those characters?

- Are there any elements or characters that exist somewhere in the middle of the masculine–feminine binary?

- What does the text communicate about queer, gay, or lesbian experience? What does the text communicate about the idea of sexual identity?

Category Description

Although many of my tenth graders avoid this category, some say to me they've been waiting for this category for a long time. This tells me that those students have wanted to discuss this aspect of texts but felt unable to do so; the arena for this discussion did not exist for them until now. The mere fact that this category exists as a scholarly lens is important for students to see, and communicates its legitimacy and contemporary significance.

I emphasize to students that gender studies focuses on gender roles in texts, and if they have an idea that doesn't exactly fit into feminist criticism, it might fit here. This category provides a space to explore all gender questions in a text, from traditional gender stereotypes to the entire gender binary. It also gives students space to consider the entire range of relationships they find in texts and experience in the world around them. This lens can certainly be used to examine contemporary literature, but it can be useful for thinking about older and even ancient literature as well as you see in the two RRs here.

Student Examples

> ### Gender Studies and Queer Theory for "Pericles' Funeral Oration" by Alex, Grade 10
>
> One aspect that really stood out to me from "Pericles' Funeral Oration" was the pressure on men to not show emotion or grieve over the death of their loved ones. Pericles doesn't offer any advice or consolation to make them feel better, he just tells them that it will be hard for them to be compared to their fathers or brothers. He says, "Everyone always speaks well of the dead and even if you rise to the greatest heights of heroism, it will be a hard thing for you to get the reputation of having come near, let alone equaled their standard" (431). The lack of emotion reminds me of the societal belief that men are considered weak if they cry. We see this a lot in modern culture, especially in the United States. It is becoming more accepted, but men and boys are still being taught that their emotions/sadness are invalid and unimportant.

O Students often use this category to note male stereotypes.

N Can you think of any texts that stand up to this stereotype?

> **Gender Studies and Queer Theory for the *Iliad* (Homer)**
> **by Masen, Grade 10**
>
> As I continue reading through the books of the *Iliad*, more and more
> evidence of a more-than-platonic relationship between Achilles and
> Patroclus appears. There is a long passage about Achilles' crushing grief
> after Patroclus' death, and an excerpt states, "he turned and twisted,
> side to side, he longed for Patroclus' manhood, his gallant heart" (pg.
> 397). I believe this grief is so intense it could not possibly be for just a
> friend. Achilles is in agony. He has lost many men in battle before but
> rarely even shed a tear. This extreme level of anguish really hints that
> Achilles and Patroclus had a deeper connection. There is mounting
> evidence to the fact that Achilles and Patroclus were in love.

N What does the text reveal about gender concepts in ancient Greece?

O Many students will use this category to speculate about a character's sexuality.

Teaching Notes

- More and more contemporary young adult fiction deals with LBQT+ experiences; if possible, keep these in your classroom library as choices for students and refer to them in examples you use.
- Whenever appropriate, point out traditional male roles and stereotypes in class texts. Feminism has received attention in popular culture, and on the RR sheet has its own category. Male stereotypes are examined less often. Create a space for this discussion in your classroom.

Critical Race Theory

Directions to Students

This theory looks at the appearance of race and racism in texts. It seeks to under-stand how minority groups are represented in texts and how cultural views of race affect them. Critical race theory scholars believe racism is a part of everyday life and want to confront it. Ask yourself:

- How is race portrayed in the text? Is this an accurate portrayal?
- How do characters of different races interact with each other? What does this reveal about the races?
- Is there evidence of systemic racism, white privilege, or microaggressions in the text? How so?

Category Description

Like the other theories, students were writing about this topic before I officially included it as a category. They would notice evidence of prejudice or racial divide in their texts and write about it as opinions or connections. Because Critical Race Theory appeared on my list after the other theories, thoughts about race sometimes fell under Marxist criticism, because race and social order are so intertwined. Including Critical Race Theory on the list gives students an opportunity to explore the history and manifestations of racism as they read about them.

In our contemporary culture, it can be difficult to talk about systemic racism and white privilege; this does not make it any less necessary. And books are the perfect scaffold to do so. Texts create a safe space to discuss these issues and we should not shy away from them. When they read, students develop empathy and understanding for others, and begin to see the worlds outside their own lives. When they write, students rehearse articulating their ideas about race, an important first step to productive conversations.

Student Examples

Critical Race Theory for *The Hate U Give* (Angie Thomas) by Mikayla, Grade 10

Starr balances two different worlds in her everyday life. She lives in a poor black neighborhood and attends a fancy rich prep school, Williamson. In the book, Starr refers to herself as either normal Starr or Williamson Starr. She makes the point to say, "Williamson Starr does not use slang . . . Williamson Starr is approachable . . . Basically, Williamson Starr doesn't give anyone a reason to call her ghetto" (71). She lives in a lower class neighborhood but attends schools with upper class kids. Her best friends attend Williamson and when news of a black teenager being shot by a cop, they automatically assume he was a drug dealer. However, as Starr knows, this is not the case. Not only is this racism but it also shows the differences of classes. Starr is stuck in the middle of this and the characters around her are all doing different things.

> N Does that perception affect Starr? How?

> N Can you find evidence of systemic racism in Starr's story?

Critical Race Theory for *The Glass Castle* (Jeannette Walls) by Eryn, Grade 10

O Eryn focuses on other groups here besides African Americans; this is an important aspect of Critical Race Theory.

N What do you mean here? What are some character traits for Rose Mary?

The Walls may be an extremely poor white family, but when they lived in the 20th century, it did not matter what they were like; people of color were still treated differently. Rose Mary being the person she is, moves them into a more lowly neighborhood, when she could have inherited a mansion from her mother. However, when describing their new home in Phoenix, Jeannette recounts "the people living on North Third Street were mostly Mexican and Indians who had moved in after the whites left for the suburbs . . . there seemed to be a couple dozen people in each house, men drinking beers from paper bags, young mothers nursing babies, and hordes of kids" (Walls 60). This small description shows how the people of different races were those more disadvantaged living on the white people's leftovers. Despite Rose Mary's views, she insists her children go to Emerson for school, in the fancy neighborhood, rather than send them to the Catholic school, where the non-white kids on their street go. She may say the nuns are a killjoy, but she is really using her white privilege to get her children into a better school, because she sees her family as superior.

O Eryn doubts the character's expressed motives and infers her real motives.

N Would you classify your descriptions here as personal racism or systemic racism? Why?

Teaching Notes

- Whenever possible, point out a text's treatment of race. Ask students: *How are characters of various races portrayed? Are there any underlying assumptions or messages here about race? Are any races conspicuously absent from this text?* However simple you make the questions, keep the conversation going. Make race part of the regular discussion of texts in your room, if it's not already.

- Many excellent shorter texts make good starting points for conversations about race. Sherman Alexie's "Indian Education," Langston Hughes' "Dream Deferred" or "I, Too, Sing America," or W.E.B. Du Bois' "On Being Crazy" are good places to start. But remember that Critical Race Theory is meant to be applied to all texts, even, or especially, texts that claim not to be about race at all.

Categories for Responding to Visual Texts

Find the Focus

Directions to Students

What is the focal point of this work? How do you know? What is the artist trying to communicate by making this point the focus? How does it relate to the rest of the piece?

Description of Category

In most paintings and photographs, the focus is easily seen. The artist *wants* us to be drawn to the focal point; our natural instincts should direct us to it. Still, students will sometimes look at a painting or picture and say they don't know what's happening in it at all. This category asks students to trust their intuition and then find evidence for it. That evidence can consist of lighting or color or positioning—whatever they find, I want students to identify some detail that supports their thinking, exactly as they must do for written texts. They are practicing the same skill.

I once attended a session run by Smithsonian American Art Museum staff at a conference. They instructed us to show students a painting and simply ask, "What do you see?" After students name elements, the teacher should ask again, "What else do you see?" The presenters told us to keep asking even after it felt like the students have named everything. In this way, students will become acquainted with a piece and will feel more comfortable making inferences about it. Tackling an entire piece of art on the first try is difficult; naming elements is easy. The simple question *What do you see?* not only builds confidence and makes for a fun whole-class activity, but also trains students to look, and look again, and look even more deeply, yet again—something they may not often do in real life.

Student Examples

Find the Focus for
Andromache Mourning Hector (Jacques-Louis David)
by Matt, Grade 10

From how I interpreted this painting I saw the focal point as Andromache. The reason for this is because it's almost like she is just sitting there still while the world goes on around her. In the background there is a dead Hector and below Andromache their child is grabbing on to her for comfort. You see her sitting there mourning while she had no control over the events happening around her. A special effect within this painting that I noticed was how the lighting over pretty much everything in the painting is dark and gloomy; however the lighting over Andromache is very bright and she is looking up into the light with a face of mourning. To me, this seems as if Andromache is looking up to the gods mourning her husband.

N How would the mood and meaning of the work be different if Hector's body were the focus?

O Matt makes an inference here that is not unfounded, based not only on the painting but our reading of the *Iliad*.

Find the Focus for
Landscape with the Fall of Icarus (Pieter Bruegel)
by Clay, Grade 10

> **N** If the farmer is not the most important, why is he the focus?

The focus of the artwork is near the center where the man is tilling his field. I think this because it is near the center and his colors are the most bright even though he isn't most important in the image. Icarus falling into the water is in the background, which was actually hard to find at first. I think that the artist did this in order to show that no one was paying attention and their lives continued normally. Daedalus isn't even in the picture and Icarus is hard to see since only half of him is visible. This part of the piece is like the rest of the artwork, everyone is minding their own business as their lives continue while Icarus is drowning to death.

> **O** Most students did not find Icarus at all until we discussed the painting in class.

> **N** Could this be related to a theme? And does it apply to real life?

Teaching Notes

- Practice will help students become more confident with this skill. A great place to begin is with Breughel's *Landscape with the Fall of Icarus* after reading Ovid's short narrative poem "Daedalus and Icarus." Breughel so obviously makes the farmer the focus and tucks the drowning Icarus in the corner. For an extra challenge with older students, read Auden's "Musée des Beaux Arts," his famous poem about this painting and the ability of humans to overlook the suffering of others.

- Often students can identify a focus but miss the meaning behind it. Paintings and photographs are like stories; they have not only moods and settings, but also themes. Ask students what the "So what?" of the painting is, just as you would a written text.

Consider the Colors

Directions to Students

What do the colors in this piece communicate? You can examine a specific color choice or the whole palette. What mood do the colors create? How do the colors relate to the theme/message of the piece?

Description of Category

In a piece of art or a photograph, perhaps the first element the viewer registers, even before the focus, is color. Colors set the mood of the piece in our minds, consciously or subconsciously. This applies to infographics as well. I want students to realize how their perceptions of the work are shaped by their reactions to the colors within it. Just as a writer crafts mood with descriptions of setting, artists craft mood with color. Students should use the "textual evidence" of color to make inferences about the work's message.

Student Examples

Consider the Colors for
Landscape with the Fall of Icarus (Pieter Bruegel)
by Masen, Grade 10

The overall color palette of this painting demonstrates a calming presence. The mood and tone of this painting are calm and they distract from the chaos of Icarus's strife. The darkness of the sea compared to the brightness of the sky and the sun demonstrate the contrast between Icarus's death and the bustling life around him. The colors are muted, except for one man in a bright red shirt, so he has become the focal point of the piece. This distracts from the image of Icarus drowning. The earthy tones of the setting make everything seem calm. The brightness of the sun creates contrast against the dark water, which is ironic, because the sun is what killed Icarus.

> **N** Based on all you have said, what do you think is the theme of this piece?

> **O** Masen touches upon the theme of the painting here.

Consider the Colors for *La Familia* (Victoria De Almeida)
by Alie, Grade 8

> N What could this symbolize?

The overall atmosphere of this painting is warm and friendly. The bright orange walls bring a feeling of warmth and happiness. The tablecloth is a rich blue, contrasting the orange and indicating that the table is the focus of the painting. Most of the people in the picture are also wearing darker colors, mostly on the cool side of the color spectrum. Through this the artist is making the people stand out. The woman on the right with a dish in her hands also seems to be important because she is the only person in the painting who is standing.

> N Why does the artist do this? Is there a theme to this painting, do you think?

> N Why is she set apart, do you think? Is there special meaning to this?

Teaching Notes

- Most textbooks have reproduced pictures and paintings within them; all trade books have some sort of cover art. Use these to ask students about color and what color communicates. Of course, use your favorite paintings and photographs as well. Some questions to consider include: *Do these colors create a feeling? Is the feeling more positive or negative? Does the feeling fit with the content of the picture? Do you think any colors contrast with each other? Is there a single color or a spot in the painting that seems different from the rest?*

Point Out the Perspective

Directions to Students

What is the perspective of this piece, and how is it important? How does the artist create the perspective? How does it relate to the mood of the piece? How does it relate to the theme?

Description of Category

This category parallels the note the narrator category for written texts—it asks students to consider the angle the "story" is viewed from. Of course, perspective can change everything, in literature and in life. I want students to realize that how they view a scene in art is not an absolute; rather, it was a deliberate choice of the artist. The artist controls our perception to shape our understanding of subject and theme. If students can recognize this in visual texts, they will better recognize it in written texts as well.

Student Examples

Point Out the Perspective for *The Great Wave Off Kanagawa* (Hokusai) by Dominick, Grade 10

> **O** Dominick links the wave to the overall mood of the painting.

The perspective of this piece is essential for creating a distinct mood for the onlooker. The wave in the top left of the painting—you can't miss it—gives an extremely daunting feeling. The viewpoint is set in such a way that makes everything around the wave seem completely insignificant and helpless. Of course, the miniscule people in the boats below are doomed by the terrifying formation, but even more intriguing is the mountain behind everything. With research, I discovered this is Mount Fuji, which is a symbol of beauty for this culture. For something so large and beautiful to look puny compared to the wave says a lot about the latter's powers.

> **N** What exactly does it say about the wave's powers in relation to Mt. Fuji?

Point Out the Perspective for *Landscape with the Fall of Icarus* (Pieter Bruegel) by Olivia, Grade 10

> **N** Could this be related to a theme?

The perspective of this painting is interesting because it is not looking directly at the situation of Daedalus and Icarus. You are looking down on an entire landscape (as the painting is titled). Icarus falling into the ocean is just a small detail of the painting; one could even miss it if they weren't looking for it. The painting almost makes the occurrence out to be insignificant in a way. Other subjects in the painting are facing the opposite way, going about their business. One motif of this piece can be the wrath of the gods when humans try to emulate them. So in this painting, the fact that Icarus is insignificant can possibly show the wishes of the gods.

> **N** Can you think of other examples of this in Greek or Roman mythology? Is this an archetypal plot?

Teaching Notes

- Differences in perspective are easy to see once you get the hang of thinking about them. Show students different pictures of the same object from varying viewpoints. For example, *The Great Wave Off Kanagawa* is part of a series of paintings titled *Thirty-Six Views of Mount Fuji*. Monet's many paintings of water lilies, or Van Gogh's series about St. Paul Asylum could also contribute to a discussion on perspective.

- You can create examples on your own as well. Take a photo of a tree outside and from normal range. Then take a photo of it from close up, from farther away, and from inside a window. Ask students the difference in mood and meaning. Have students take their own photos to illustrate differences in perspective.

References

Alexander, Patricia A. 2012. "Reading into the Future: Competence for the 21st Century." *Educational Psychologist* 47 (4): 259–80.

Atwell, Nancie. 1998. *In the Middle: New Understandings About Writing, Reading, and Learning*. Portsmouth, NH: Boynton/Cook.

Brizee, Allen, J. Case Tompkins, Libby Chernouski, Elizabeth Boyle, and Sebastian Williams. 2015. "Literary Theory and Schools of Criticism." Purdue Online Writing Lab. https://owl.english.purdue.edu/owl/resource/722/1/.

Carretti, Barbara, Nadia Caldarola, Chiara Tencati, and Cesare Cornoldi. 2014. "Improving Reading Comprehension in Reading and Listening Settings: The Effect of Two Training Programmes Focusing on Metacognition and Working Memory." *British Journal of Educational Psychology* 84 (2): 194–210.

Ericsson, K. Anders, Michael J. Prietula, and Edward T. Cokely. 2007. "The Making of an Expert." *Harvard Business Review*. https://hbr.org/2007/07/the-making-of-an-expert.

Fisher, Douglas, Nancy Frey, and Diane Lapp. 2012. *Teaching Students to Read Like Detectives*. Bloomington, IN: Solution Tree Press.

Frey, Nancy, and Douglas Fisher. 2013. *Rigorous Reading: 5 Access Point for Comprehending Complex Texts*. Thousand Oaks, CA: Corwin.

Gallagher, Kelly. 2009. *Readicide*. Portland, ME: Stenhouse.

———. 2011. *Write Like This*. Portland, ME: Stenhouse.

———. 2016. "Exploration, risk, and failure are essential components in a writer's growth. Exploration and risk will not occur if everything is graded." Twitter. November 28, 5:25 pm. https://twitter.com/KellyGToGo/status/803409450547617793.

Hinton, S. E. 2006. *The Outsiders*. New York: Penguin.

Locke, John. 2017. "John Locke." *The Book Lover's Enchiridion: Thoughts on the Solace and Companionship of Books*, edited by Alexander Ireland, 61. London, UK: Forgotten Books.

Magno, Carlo. 2010. "The Role of Metacognitive Skills in Developing Critical Thinking." *Metacognition and Learning* 5 (2): 137–56. https://link.springer.com/article/10.1007/s11409-010-9054-4.

Murray, Donald. 1990. *Shoptalk*. Portsmouth, NH: Heinemann.

O'Reilley, Mary R. 1998. *Radical Presence: Teaching as Contemplative Practice*. Portsmouth, NH: Heinemann.

Patall, Erika A., Harrison Cooper, and Jorgianne C. Robinson. 2008. "The Effects of Choice on Intrinsic Motivation and Related Outcomes: A Meta-Analysis of Research Findings." *Psychological Bulletin* 134 (2): 270–300.

Patall, Erika. A., Harris Cooper, and Susan. R. Wynn. 2010. "The Effectiveness and Relative Importance of Choice in the Classroom." *Journal of Educational Psychology* 102 (4): 896–915.

Rosenblatt, Louise. 2005. *Making Meaning with Texts: Selected Essays*. Portsmouth, NH: Heinemann.

Sulzer, Mark. 2014. "The Common Core State Standards and the 'Basalisation' of Youth." *English Teaching: Practice and Critique* 13 (1): 134–54.

Yolen, Jane. 2007. For Writers. *Jane Yolen*. http://janeyolen.com/for-writers/.

———. 2016. Jane Yolen: Quotes. *Goodreads*. https://www.goodreads.com/author/quotes/5989.Jane_Yolen.

Zinsser, William. 2006. *On Writing Well*. New York: HarperCollins.